AF745288

REFUGE AUSTRALIA
AUSTRALIA'S HUMANITARIAN RECORD

Klaus Neumann is a German-born historian currently based in Melbourne. Recent work includes the book, *Shifting Memories: The Nazi Past in the New Germany* (University of Michigan Press, 2000), and the radio play, *A Doubtful Character* (broadcast in Australia and New Zealand in 2003 and 2004). He intends to follow up *Refuge Australia* with a more comprehensive account of Australian responses to refugees.

BRIEFINGS

A series of topical books exploring social, political and cultural issues in contemporary Australia

Series editors: Peter Browne and Julian Thomas
Australian Policy Online (www.apo.org.au)
Institute for Social Research, Swinburne University of Technology

Also in this series

America's Pie: Trade and Culture Since 9/11
by Jock Given

Slapping on the Writs:
Defamation, Developers and Community Activism
by Brian Walters

Mr Ruddock Goes to Geneva
by Spencer Zifcak

Sexing it Up: Iraq, Intelligence and Australia
by Geoffrey Barker

Rebels With a Cause: Independents in Australian Politics
by Brian Costar & Jennifer Curtin

Refuge Australia

AUSTRALIA'S HUMANITARIAN RECORD

KLAUS NEUMANN

UNSW
PRESS

A UNSW Press book

Published by
University of New South Wales Press Ltd
University of New South Wales
Sydney NSW 2052
AUSTRALIA
www.unswpress.com.au

© Klaus Neumann 2004
First published 2004

This book is copyright. Apart from any fair dealing for the purpose of private study, research, criticism or review, as permitted under the Copyright Act, no part may be reproduced by any process without written permission. Enquiries should be addressed to the publisher.

National Library of Australia
Cataloguing-in-Publication entry

Neumann, Klaus, 1958– .

Refuge Australia: Australia's humanitarian record.

ISBN 0 86840 711 9

1. Refugees – Australia – History – 20th century. 2. Immigrants – Australia – History – 20th century. 3. Australia – Emigration and immigration – History – 20th century. I. Title. (Series: Briefings series).

305.906910994

The writing of this book was supported by the Myer Foundation through A Just Australia

Cover photograph: Polish stowaway released, August 1941, Argus Newspaper Collection of Photographs, State Library of Victoria

Edited by Kate Manton

Printed by BPA Digital

Contents

Introduction

Wong Fun Cheung was held in a Sydney detention centre awaiting deportation. Through a lawyer, he applied for political asylum on the grounds that he feared he would be executed if forced to return home.[1] While there was no evidence to prove his fear was well founded, it was known that Wong's government, which Australia did not recognise, had scant regard for human rights. "I do not see this as a case for political asylum. Certainly the applicant did not come here as a refugee of a political kind," the minister responsible for asylum requests decided.[2] In an appeal to the authorities, Wong's lawyer conceded that his client was an illegal immigrant and that "any decision to allow him to remain in the country would be an act of mercy by the Government."[3] But the government was not to let humanitarian considerations weaken its resolve to deport illegals. In a Cabinet submission, Alexander Downer made it clear that the government's stance was to send a signal to those behind the "well organised traffic in illegal entry."[4] In parliament, he claimed that Wong and his compatriots were "past masters at the art of evasion and of avoiding rules relating to immigration laid down not only by this country but also by other countries."[5]

The small band of refugees – six men, sixteen women and 34 children – had finally reached Australian territory. They tried to justify their illegal entry to the government official interviewing them. One day, soldiers had come to their village, killed a young man, burned down their houses, destroyed their food gardens and killed their livestock.

They had been accused of assisting dissidents, a claim they vehemently denied. After hiding for several months in the bush, they eventually returned to their village and rebuilt it, only to be revisited by the soldiers. It was then that they decided to head to Australian territory. The Australian official thought this information was "probably true" but was unable to confirm it.[6] Further enquiries revealed that the unlawful entrants were not seeking political asylum but a "haven."[7] Under instructions to remove bogus refugees from Australian territory, the official had them sent back across the border. Given that the escorts accompanying them to the edge of Australian territory were armed, the refugees had little choice but to do as they were told, regardless of their fear of the military in their own country.

Australia offered Samad Abdul bin Amjah a place of refuge when war made it impossible for him to live in his homeland. More than four years later, the Minister for Immigration told Amjah to leave because the situation in his country of origin had changed for the better. By then he had settled in Sydney, married an Australian, and fathered two children. An appeal for leniency by his employer, who offered to guarantee a bond should Amjah be allowed to stay, failed to persuade the minister. Amjah's wife, Mavis, was free to accompany her husband but, conscious of the conditions in his homeland, she did not want to risk her own and her young children's health and safety. A couple of months after his enforced return, Amjah wrote in despair to an Australian diplomat: "I am appealing to you to place before the authorities a request that I should be permitted to return to Australia so that I can be with my family. My wife is pregnant, so you can imagine my anxiety."[8]

•

These three stories sound familiar enough: the deportation of illegal immigrants whose claims for asylum have been rejected; the forced removal of refugees before they could lodge a claim for asylum; and the deportation of people whose temporary protection visas have not been renewed. They represent the harsh reality of post-*Tampa* Australia.

It may come as a surprise, then, that the cases behind these three stories are not from the early twenty-first century. Wong Fun Cheung was a Chinese stowaway, who was threatened with deportation to the

People's Republic of China via Hong Kong in 1962. Although Australia did not have diplomatic relations with China, it had previously deported men there to deter other would-be illegal immigrants. (The Alexander Downer in the first story was the then Minister for Immigration and the father of the current Minister for Foreign Affairs.) The second story relates an incident in March 1971 in the West Sepik District of the Australian Territory of Papua and New Guinea. Between 1963 and 1973, Australian patrol officers returned hundreds of West Papuans, who had sought refuge in Papua and New Guinea, to Indonesian-controlled West Irian (Irian Jaya). Samad Abdul bin Amjah, from the third tale, whose story has been the subject of an SBS television documentary, was a Malayan who came to Australia as a so-called wartime refugee in 1943. Like others in his situation, in 1947 he was put on a ship to Singapore.

I am telling these stories partly to sound a note of caution. Before the 1990s, Australian responses to refugees and asylum seekers were not as generous as both the Howard government and many refugee advocacy groups have been suggesting. But that is not to say that the current government's hardline policies represent business as usual. Not even the three earlier stories provide unequivocal evidence for parallels between the 1940s, 1950s and 1960s on the one hand, and the post-*Tampa* years on the other.

Wong Fun Cheung was spared the fate of other deportees who had been returned to China. His case came before Cabinet just after another deportation to China had created an outcry in the Australian press. Then, two prominent Liberal Party backbenchers had intimated that they were prepared to cross the floor over the issue and thereby deprive the government of its two-seat majority. Cabinet's decision to back down was also influenced by an offer from Formosa's government to resettle Wong and other Chinese deportees. Although nothing came of that offer, four years later Cabinet quietly agreed to allow Wong and others in his situation to remain in Australia.[9]

While the West Papuan refugees mentioned earlier were returned to Indonesian territory, they would have been able to cross the border again elsewhere. At the time, Australian officials were more likely to tolerate their presence in camps on the Australian side of the border than to hand them over to the Indonesian military.

Soon after his arrival in Singapore, Amjah signed on as crew on a cargo vessel bound for Australia. In Sydney, he jumped ship. He was arrested, given a dictation test in French, charged with being a prohibited immigrant, and convicted. When he appealed, the judge found that the government had had no right to make him leave Australia in the first place. The Attorney-General's Department advised against pursuing the matter further and Amjah remained in Australia.[10]

Australia's record of dealing with refugees and asylum seekers does not easily support either the view that current Australian policies are merely a continuation of a previous hard-hearted approach to those seeking our protection, or the argument that they are an aberration within a tradition of generosity. But then, the retrospective search for pedigrees often does little to enhance our understanding of either the past or the present. Histories that quarry the past merely to establish genealogies suited for political point-scoring tend to lack complexity and have little analytical value.

Maybe the glaring contradictions in past policies, and their apparent refusal either to endorse or condemn present policies, explain why there as so few histories of Australian responses to refugees and asylum seekers. For it is astounding that the debate about current Australian refugee policies has not spawned detailed histories of their antecedents.

The past and the present are often incompatible, and therefore past and present policies are not necessarily readily comparable. The end of the Cold War brought about a dramatic shift in the world's refugee movements and, more importantly, in the West's response to refugees. No longer were Eastern European refugees welcomed as immigrants by the "Free World." Refugees after 1990 are far more likely to have been repatriated than permanently resettled; and European countries, Canada, the United States and Australia have tried to make their borders impenetrable, thus preventing refugees from seeking asylum. On several occasions since the early 1990s, the United Nations High Commissioner for Refugees (UNHCR) and the United States and its allies have intervened in conflicts in order to contain refugee movements. Despite these conspicuous changes, histories of past Australian responses to refugees could inform and advance current debates. By exploring, for example, what motivated government policies in the past, such histories could illuminate aspects of current policies that would otherwise appear self-evident.

This book tries to contribute to an informed historical perspective, even though it is deliberately selective in its approach and cannot make up for the lack of detailed histories. By examining a variety of historical cases, it emphasises the benefits of a critical investigation of Australia's past. Such an investigation is not driven by the aim to justify or condemn the present, but by the idea that from the viewpoint of the past, the present is but one possible outcome. From this perspective, alternatives to the current refugee and asylum seeker regime are conceivable. Going back in time offers us the opportunity to take a long look at the present and to let ourselves be startled by its peculiarity, and perhaps allows us to think about and work towards alternatives that are not merely variations of the current approach.

This critical investigation is not a contribution to a black-armband view of past Australian responses to refugees and asylum seekers. Admittedly, my history suggests that Australians ought to be less proud of their country's record than has generally been the case. Yet my aim is not to prompt an acknowledgement of a hitherto hidden and shameful past. Rather, I am interested in imagining alternatives to the present refugee and asylum seeker regime. Surprising as it may sound, given the amount of attention it has received in the Australian media, much of this regime still needs to be properly understood and acknowledged, rather than taken as a given. A proper acknowledgement would entail an exploration of its historical baggage – beyond its presumed foundations in the mid 1970s or early 1990s.

Almost all attempts to make sense of the historical origins of the current asylum seeker and refugee policies have focused on the 1990s. Certainly, most analysts have paid some attention to the period from the arrival of the first Indochinese "boat people" in 1976 to the passing of the Migration Reform Act in 1992, but there has been almost no mention of what happened earlier. A report by Charles Price, commissioned by the National Population Council for its 1991 Refugee Review, is the only notable exception.[11] This book tries to redress this imbalance and as such is exclusively concerned with what occurred before 1973.

This cut-off date is not arbitrary. It marks a turning point in several respects. In 1973, Australia withdrew its support for the Intergovernmental Committee for European Migration, which had been set up to facilitate the resettlement of European refugees. Through the Intergovernmental Committee, the United States, Australia and other Western countries had often been able to bypass the UNHCR. In 1973, the Whitlam government formally abolished the White Australia policy, which had played a significant role in shaping Australia's refugee policy. At the end of 1973, Papua New Guinea was granted self-government, and the refugees who had been arriving in the Australian Territory of Papua and New Guinea since the early 1960s effectively became the responsibility of the Papua New Guinean government.

Also in 1973, Australia acceded to the 1967 Protocol Relating to the Status of Refugees. The 1951 United Nations Convention Relating to the Status of Refugees defines a refugee as a person who:

> owing to well-founded fear of being persecuted for reasons of race, religion, nationality, membership of a particular social group or political opinion, is outside the country of his nationality and is unable or, owing to such fear, is unwilling to avail himself of the protection of that country; or who, not having a nationality and being outside the country of his former habitual residence... is unable or, owing to such fear, is unwilling to return to it.

On its own, the Convention applied only to people who became refugees as a result of events that had occurred before 1 January 1951. Further, signatories had the option of limiting their obligations to European refugees. Australia exercised that option when it ratified the Convention in 1954. The 1967 Protocol removed the Convention's geographical and time limitations. It was only when Australia acceded to the Protocol that it accepted obligations under international law regarding refugees other than European displaced persons (DPs) and so-called escapees. These obligations include the commitment not to return ("*refouler*") a refugee "to the frontiers of territories where his life or freedom would be threatened on account of his race, religion, nationality, membership of a particular social group or political opinion."

The 1951 Convention was drafted with a particular group of people – Eastern European refugees – in mind, and against the backdrop of the Cold War. In recent years, refugee advocates have often used the fact that Australia is a party to the Convention to argue that it has *legal* obligations vis-à-vis those who arrive on its shores to seek asylum. I consider such a line of argument, while undoubtedly correct in principle, to be unnecessarily legalistic. Instead I ask whether or not Australia has *moral* obligations towards those seeking asylum. In the context of this question, it is particularly instructive to explore Australia's response to refugees and asylum seekers before 1973, when it was under hardly any international legal obligation to process or accept asylum seekers.

Drawing on published and unpublished sources from the late 1930s to the early 1970s, I try to debunk four assumptions about Australia's responses to refugees and asylum seekers in the past. The first of these is frequently espoused by advocates of the current policy of deterrence, but equally by many of its detractors:

Traditionally, Australia has accepted more than its fair share of refugees from around the world.

The other assumptions do not feature as prominently in either justifications or criticisms of the current policy, but they, too, have informed much of the public discourse on Australian refugee and asylum seeker policies. They also tend to be uncontested and seemingly do not warrant specific historical evidence in their support:

Australia did not have to deal with onshore asylum seekers until the arrival of the first Indochinese boat people in 1976.

Australia has always supported international legal instruments for the protection of refugees and worked closely with the UNHCR to alleviate the suffering of refugees across the globe.

The forcible repatriation of refugees and the granting of temporary protection visas are measures pioneered by the Howard government in response to the arrival of boat people in the late 1990s.

This book critically examines these assumptions.

The following seven chapters sketch a history. They also tell stories – such as those with which I began this introduction. Because of the lack of detailed historical studies of Australia's refugee and asylum seeker policies before the mid 1970s – only Australia's response to Jewish refugees has been exhaustively analysed – my findings are largely based on original archival research. Many of the documents I examined in the course of my research had never before been sighted by a historian. I have quoted some of them at length to let them speak for themselves and occasionally to give readers the opportunity to engage with the evidence rather than with my summaries of it.

Because the archival documents I draw on are often about individual lives and tend to deal with specific instances of decision making, I felt some of them should be given narrative life. Stories, and the dwelling on specific people and events, also act as important reminders: a book about refugee policies and their administration could easily obscure the fact that these policies – however much they are informed by global politics or collective angst – affect, indeed often save or destroy, the lives of individuals.

I take issue with commentators – on all sides of the political divide – who make rhetorical use of the past in order to condemn or justify current policies. Arguing for a thorough investigation of Australia's past and committed to writing histories that have integrity, I have endeavoured to bring my skills as a professional historian to the task. Even so, my investigation has not been disinterested, as I am hoping the history told in this book will intervene, however modestly, in the current debate about Australia's response to "non-citizens" who seek its protection.

CHAPTER 1

Reffos

Refugees made their homes in Australia throughout the first three and a half decades of the twentieth century. Approximately 2000 Jews, escaping anti-Semitism in Poland and other Eastern European countries, immigrated during the 1920s. A similar number of so-called White Russians – followers of the Tsar who had fled the Soviet Union after the defeat of the counter-revolutionary armies in the early 1920s – arrived between 1920 and 1940. Many anti-fascists who had felt compelled to leave Italy after Mussolini came to power were among the 23,233 Italians who migrated to Australia between 1922 and 1930.[1]

To the Australian authorities at this time it did not matter why people wanting to settle in Australia left their home countries. There were no specific provisions for refugees in the regulations governing permanent entry. Attempts in the 1920s to lobby for a quota for Jewish refugees failed. Prospective immigrants, whatever the reason for their desire to migrate to Australia, needed only to comply with the White Australia policy (which essentially meant that they had to be of European ancestry). During the 1930s, all non-British immigrants also required landing permits: these permits were usually only issued to applicants who had been nominated by an Australian resident or who had landing money. Immigrants from Britain often had access to assisted passages, and were thus further privileged over other Europeans. The proportion of migrants from outside the British Isles was very small, and their impact on the overall composition of Australia's population negligible. In 1939, only 2 per cent of the non-indigenous population was not of Anglo-Celtic ancestry.

Prospective immigrants not seeking refuge were only drawn to Australia when its economy was flourishing. During the first half of the 1930s, Australia held few attractions and, over a five-year period, permanent departures exceeded permanent arrivals by almost 20,000.[2] The Department of the Interior tried to regulate the level of immigration depending on the state of the economy and Australia's perceived capacity to absorb migrants. During the depression of the 1930s, for example, assisted passages became unavailable. After 1932, the department controlled the number of landing permits by varying the amount of landing money required.

Until the mid 1930s, Australia had been able to ignore major refugee movements. Only a small proportion of Europe's refugees had wanted to settle in Australia, not least because they had other, more attractive, options. Most Eastern European Jews, for example, emigrated to Western Europe and the United States; comparatively few attempted to come to Australia. But Germany's neighbours were reluctant to accommodate Hitler's political opponents, and even more reluctant to welcome large numbers of German and Austrian Jews. The historian Andrew Markus reports that by May 1938, "Australia House in London was receiving 300 applications per week, covering approximately twice this number of persons; by August applications reached 500 per week."[3]

In mid 1938, unemployment was once again low. The country had evidently recovered from the depression. Net immigration was well below pre-depression levels, and Australia's comparatively low population density was perceived as a problem. In September 1938, the governor-general, Lord Gowrie, insisted that Australia must "populate or perish": "Australians are living in a fool's paradise; the overpopulated nations of the world are turning their greedy and hungry eyes... on this great undeveloped country."[4] Did the Australian government therefore consider refugee immigration a welcome bonus? Did it lower the amount of landing money required to make it easier for refugees to immigrate? On the contrary: in June 1938, Cabinet, worried about the potentially high level of Jewish immigration, agreed on an annual ceiling of 5100 Jewish immigrants per year. In order to identify Jewish applicants, the Department of the Interior amended application forms for prospective immigrants. Applicants were now required to state whether or not they belonged to the Jewish race.

Australia was not alone in asking prospective immigrants whether or not they were Jewish. Nor was the Australian practice singularly perfidious. In 1938, the top Swiss police officer expressed his concern that, given the flight of thousands of refugees across the German–Swiss border, Switzerland would become "saturated with Jews."[5] On behalf of his government, he sought the help of the Nazi authorities in distinguishing between bona fide German tourists and Jewish refugees. In response to his request, the Germans stamped the passports of people classified as Jews with a red "J." From October 1938, holders of these specially marked passports needed a visa to enter Switzerland, whereas no such requirement applied to other Germans. While this measure effectively restricted the entry of German Jews into Switzerland, Australia's practice was less effectual, as not all refugees disclosed their "race" in their visa applications.

In March 1938, the United States president, Franklin Roosevelt, called for an international conference to consider the issue of German refugees, and to identify a solution for the considerable number of German and Austrian Jews who were desperate to leave but could not find a sanctuary. In July 1938, delegations from 32 countries met in the French resort of Evian-les-Bains. All delegates stressed that their governments were already doing a great deal to assist the refugees, and tried to justify their existing quotas. Thomas Walter White, Minister for Trade and Customs in the Lyons government, represented Australia at the conference. After pointing out that Australia was already doing its fair share he said:

> Under the circumstances, Australia cannot do more, for it will be appreciated that in a young country man power from the source from which most of its citizens have sprung is preferred, while undue privileges cannot be given to one particular class of non-British subjects without injustice to others. It will no doubt be appreciated also that, as we have no real racial problem, we are not desirous of importing one by encouraging any scheme of large-scale foreign migration.[6]

White's argument in defence of his government's inaction was at best curious: he seemed to suggest that the privileging of refugees over other immigrants was an injustice so great that it outweighed that suffered by people who were forced to flee their homes.

The conference ended in failure. Only one country, the Dominican Republic, invited refugees to come. Evian confirmed what German and Austrian refugees already knew only too well: that they were not welcome outside Germany, however much the Hitler government tried to make them leave, and that several borders had been altogether closed to them. The only tangible result of the gathering in Evian was the establishment of the Intergovernmental Committee on Refugees. Its brief was to identify resettlement options for refugees and negotiate with the German government for an orderly departure programme for Jews. Its immediate impact was minimal, however, because the German authorities were uncooperative, and because until 1943 the committee's budget covered only its administrative costs.

The Australian government's reluctance to accept large numbers of Jewish refugees stemmed from prejudices similar to those informing Nazi racial policies. For many of Australia's leaders, to be Jewish meant to be a member of the Jewish "race" – rather than to belong to the Jewish faith, or to have been classified by the Nazis as Jewish on account of being a descendant of someone belonging to the Jewish faith. When White warned against the importation of a racial problem, he evidently had Jewish (rather than German or Austrian) immigrants in mind.

The government of Joseph Lyons had also been remarkably tolerant of Hitler's Germany. Professing to respect the sovereignty of Germany, it had not raised its voice against Hitler's racist policies and the murders committed by his henchmen. It had done little to prohibit Nazi propaganda in Australia but instead had protected Germany against anti-fascist agitation. The Czech anti-fascist writer, Egon Erwin Kisch, was declared a prohibited immigrant when he attempted to land in Australia in 1934. Like his British counterpart, Lyons believed in the appeasement strategy.

The government's approach towards German refugees was contested, however, even in its own ranks. Stanley Bruce had been prime minister from 1923 to 1929 and became Australia's high commissioner to Britain in 1933. During the 1930s, he regularly represented Australia at the League of Nations annual assembly. The historian Michael Blakeney writes that Bruce "became probably the best informed Australian on European affairs."[7] On 17 November 1938, he urged the Australian government to increase its number of Jewish refugees significantly, and to make this increase the subject of a public announcement. He argued that such an announcement "would greatly increase, particularly in the United States, the goodwill towards and the prestige of Australia."[8]

Bruce also responded to the *Reichskristallnacht* pogroms that month, when well-organised bands of Nazi paramilitaries set fire to synagogues all over Germany. The pressure on Jews to emigrate increased; many Jewish men were imprisoned in concentration camps and only released once their families had made arrangements to leave Germany. Bruce suggested that Australia accept 30,000 refugees over a three-year period, and cabled a draft statement to that effect to Canberra. The Lyons government halved the figure put forward by Bruce, but followed his advice to make its acceptance of the refugees public. While emphasising Australia's generosity, the announcement merely confirmed the status quo: the target of 15,000 over three years was in fact slightly lower than that of 5100 Jewish immigrants per year, which had been set, but not publicised, a few months earlier.

On 1 December 1938, the Minister for the Interior, John McEwen, announced:

> The Government feels that, if a solution of [the refugee] problem is to be found, countries must be prepared to receive a proportion of those to be expatriated, in relation to the capacity of the countries to assimilate them... In arriving at the figure of 15,000 over a period of three years, the Government has been influenced by the necessity that the existing standards of living should not be disturbed and for reconciling with the interests of refugees, the interests of Australia's present population, and of the people of British race who desire to establish themselves in Australia.[9]

McEwen copied the above passage from Bruce's draft statement, and then added his own qualifiers. He made it clear that Australia's approach to European refugees would be subordinate to its immigration policy:

> Although the refugee problem is one quite apart from the general question of immigration, in that it deals with the specific question of the amelioration of the conditions of oppressed people, at the same time it is essential that it should be considered in relation to the general question of immigration so far as the Commonwealth is concerned. The Government has decided, therefore, that, on broad lines, the admission of refugees should conform to the same principles as those governing the entry of white aliens generally.[10]

Thus, although the government introduced a quota, its response did not take into account the difference between refugees and other immigrants. In fact, it deliberately ignored this difference and decided that refugees would be admitted on the basis of their usefulness for Australia and suitability as settlers rather than any personal need:

> Desperate as is the need of many of these unfortunate people, it is not the intention of the Government to issue permits for entry influenced by the necessity of individual cases. On the contrary, it is felt that it will be possible for Australia to play its part amongst the nations of the world, in absorbing its reasonable quota of these people, while at the same time selecting those who will become valuable citizens of Australia and, we trust, patriots of their new home, without this action disturbing industrial conditions in Australia.[11]

The quota in effect limited refugee arrivals by stipulating that only a certain number meeting the usual requirements would be admitted. In 1938 and 1939, far more eligible refugees applied to migrate to Australia than were permitted to immigrate as part of the quota. According to the historian Paul Bartrop, in late 1938 only ten per cent of applications from non-guaranteed refugees were accepted, while many of those rejected met the Australian requirements.[12] In 1939, the government made small amendments to the target of 15,000 arrivals over three years. It agreed to admit 500 parents of Jewish immigrants outside the quota, and an additional 1000 Jews in

1939. Throughout, the Labor Party opposition supported the government's policy.

On 1 September 1939, Germany invaded Poland. Two days later, Australia declared war on Germany. The war brought Australia's efforts to resettle refugees from Nazi Germany largely to an end. German nationals became enemy aliens, regardless of whether they were refugees or loyal citizens of Nazi Germany. With a few exceptions, only refugees who had left Germany before the war and who had already obtained Australian landing permits were allowed to proceed to Australia.

•

There are conflicting estimates of the total number of European refugees who arrived in Australia in 1938 and 1939. The Minister for Immigration told parliament after the war that 1556 refugees arrived in Australia in 1938, and 5080 in 1939.[13] But these figures include only immigrants who could be identified as refugees on account of information contained in their visa applications. There were undoubtedly others who met the usual entry requirements and were classified as ordinary immigrants. The Commonwealth statistician counted 2251 German, 78 Czech and Slovakian, and 44 Austrian nationals arriving in 1938; and 5583 German, 354 Czech and Slovakian, and 1016 Polish arrivals in 1939.[14] The overwhelming majority of these would have been permanent refugee arrivals. Taking also into account a small number of refugee arrivals for the period 1933 to 1937 and the war years, Australia's total intake of people fleeing Nazi Germany or the territories occupied by it was somewhere in the vicinity of 10,000.

In excess of this, more than 2000 refugees arrived as internees courtesy of the British government, which evacuated internees to Canada and Australia during the war. The overwhelming majority of the enemy aliens interned by British authorities in Britain and Malaya, and sent to Australia aboard the *Dunera* and *Queen Mary* in 1940, were Jews who had fled Germany and Austria in the late 1930s. Many of them settled in Australia.

The question of whether Australia's response to those fleeing Nazi Germany was mean or generous has been intensely debated. Answers have depended on the criteria used to evaluate that response. Should

Australia's effort be measured in relation to the responses of other countries? Or should it be assessed in the light of its capacity to accommodate refugees?

Those looking to other countries to gauge Australia's commitment find it reasonable. Comparable countries such as New Zealand and South Africa only admitted a few token refugees. Canada's immigration authorities tried to keep Jews out altogether:[15] only Jewish farmers in possession of a substantial amount of capital were issued visas. It was with reluctance that the Canadian government even sent a delegation to Evian. In June 1939, the government was asked to allow passengers from the *St. Louis*, a ship carrying 907 German Jews who had been turned away by Cuban authorities, to disembark in Canada. The head of the immigration department claimed that no country could "open its doors wide enough to take in the hundreds of thousands of Jewish people who want to leave Europe: the line must be drawn somewhere."[16] The *St. Louis* was forced to return to Germany, where many of its passengers perished. The prejudices and fears of Canada's politicians more than matched those of Thomas Walter White and others like him in Australia. In March 1938, the Canadian prime minister, Mackenzie King, noted in his diary his conviction that it was crucial "to keep this part of the Continent free from unrest and from too great an intermixture of foreign strains of blood," and that nothing would be gained "by creating an internal problem in an effort to meet an international one."[17]

But how fruitful is it to point out that other countries behaved less ethically than Australia? What is to be gained from stressing Australia's comparative generosity, in 1938 or in 2004, when the benchmark is so low? What can be gained from emphasising a global zeitgeist that condones anti-Semitism, anti-alienism or collective egotism?

Those depicting Australia's response in a favourable light point out that its refugee intake was generous on a per capita basis. But Australia's capacity was greater than that of other nations precisely because of its small population. During the 1920s, Australia had absorbed a substantial number of immigrants annually – comparatively more than some other New World countries, and far more than Germany's European neighbours. The economy was geared towards significant net immigration gains. Australia's capacity to accommodate a large number of immigrants during periods of economic prosperity was well established.

Regardless of whether or not it was generous, Australia's response to the refugee crisis created by the Nazis' policies marked an important turning point. For the first time, an Australian government made special provisions for the admission of refugees (even though they may have had the effect of restricting rather than facilitating refugee immigration). For the first time, the Australian public was involved in a vigorous debate about the merits of resettling refugees. Even a plan to create a settlement for 50,000 Jewish refugees in the Kimberleys, which was floated between 1938 and 1944, was taken seriously both by the government and the public. But at no stage in these discussions about refugee immigration, be it in newspaper editorials or in Cabinet, was the issue of admitting refugees out of humanitarian concern uncoupled from the issue of immigration.

•

While the Australian government made special provisions for those fleeing Nazi Germany, it was less moved by the plight of other European refugees. In 1938 and 1939, the government received many representations on behalf of Spaniards loyal to the republic who had fled across the border to France, where they were accommodated in refugee camps. In numerical terms, the Spanish refugee crisis was, at that time, at least on a par with that created by Nazi Germany: by early 1939, 450,000 Spanish refugees had crossed the border, more than had fled Germany, Austria and Czechoslovakia between 1933 and 1938.

Cabinet decided that "no special action was to be taken to encourage Spanish refugees"; instead, each application was decided on its merits provided that the applicant met the usual requirements: £200 or, if the applicant had a guarantor in Australia, £50 landing money.[18] A mere 24 Spanish nationals were admitted to Australia in 1939.[19] The government also rejected a suggestion by the Australasian Council of Trade Unions and others that Australia should provide "financial assistance with a view of transporting these unfortunate people to countries which are prepared to give them asylum,"[20] and decided not to add to a £3000 contribution to the Spanish refugee relief effort, which it had allocated in 1938.

In February 1939, the Department of the Interior defined refugees as "persons of German nationality, or former Austrian or German nationality, or of Czechoslovakian or former Czechoslovakian nationality, against whom there is political discrimination."[21] Such a narrow, specific definition was in line with those previously adopted by the League of Nations. Australia did not recognise a generic set of conditions that rendered somebody a refugee. Nevertheless, some refugees who did not conform to the department's definition still managed to migrate to Australia. Emery Barcs, for example, who later achieved prominence working for the Australian Broadcasting Commission, lost his job as a journalist in his native Hungary after his government introduced its own racial laws in April 1938. Together with his wife Vica, Barcs successfully applied for an Australian landing permit and left Europe in July 1939. He was a refugee, but he could also represent himself as the Australian correspondent for several European newspapers, and thus a migrant to Australia for professional reasons.[22]

Jewish refugees arriving in the late 1930s were expected to settle in Australia. I have found no evidence to suggest that their stay was thought to be anything but permanent, irrespective of whether or not the political conditions that forced them to flee were to change. The situation was different for a small number of Polish refugees who had fled to Japan. Most of them had escaped to Lithuania in 1939, and then obtained transit visas for Japan in the unlikely hope that they would proceed from there to the Dutch colonies of Surinam or Curaçao, which were the last destinations a refugee could reach without first procuring a visa. Once the Polish refugees arrived in Japan, the Japanese authorities insisted they move on, but most had nowhere to go. In April 1941, the Menzies government decided to accept a small number of them. But unlike the German and Austrian refugees who had reached Australia in 1939, the Poles (most of them Jewish) were only "admitted for the duration of the war."[23] Altogether, 83 Polish refugees from Japan were given temporary sanctuary in Australia.

During the war, Australia also admitted about 15,000 so-called wartime refugees from Southeast Asia. Some of them were evacuated from Dutch or British colonies threatened by the Japanese; others were seamen stranded in Australia after the fall of Singapore. They included more than 5000 Asians, whose stay in Australia was always intended to be strictly temporary. I discuss their case in more detail in Chapter 7.

•

So far, I have been mainly concerned with Australian government policies. How, though, did the Australian public respond to refugees? And how did the government in turn take into account popular opinion? In the late 1930s, organisations such as the Victorian International Refugee Council and the Sydney-based European Emergency Committee lobbied the government on behalf of European refugees. But they did not represent the majority of the electorate. Before the *Reichskristallnacht* pogroms of November 1938, most Australians were at best sceptical about the admission of thousands of refugees, who were often derogatorily referred to as "reffos"; but the pogroms triggered a wave of sympathy for German Jews. A report by one of Australia's domestic intelligence agencies noted on 21 November that "most Australians [now] take an extremely broad-minded view" towards the immigration of Jewish refugees.[24] But this shift in public opinion was largely temporary. The government knew that many Australians were essentially opposed to the arrival of refugees. Its decision to limit Australia's intake to 15,000 over three years may have been a response to the electorate's latent xenophobia as much as a reflection of the government's own anti-alienism.

The government neither actively encouraged anti-alienist sentiment, nor did it set out to convince the electorate of the potential value of refugees as immigrants and new citizens. Rather, it tried to keep the issue out of the public's eye as much as possible. John McEwen's announcement regarding the admission of 15,000 refugees was an exception. Otherwise, throughout the late 1930s, the government did not usually publicise decisions about the admission of refugees. When it did make announcements, they were intended to soothe a nervous Australian public. In February 1939, for example, the Department of the Interior assured Australians that, while it had been flooded by 40,000 applications in recent months, it was hand-picking refugee migrants. A newspaper article summarised the department's position:

> Unless a male refugee applicant is a skilled worker, particularly in a branch of industry in which there is a shortage, he has little hope of getting a permit if he possesses only the minimum landing money. The Department has almost reached the stage where it can restrict permits to Jewish and other refugees, who can produce proof of possessing many hundreds, or even thousands of pounds... Middle-aged and elderly refugees are being admitted only in exceptional cases.[25]

The actual arrival of Jewish refugees was organised to attract as little public attention as possible. There were no welcoming ceremonies for ships carrying refugees (as there would be ten years later). On 9 November 1938, the government cabled the Australian high commissioner in London regarding earlier advice that not more than twenty refugees were to arrive in Australia by any one ship:

> Position is that number of permits to enter Australia have been granted to refugees and consequently if large numbers holding valid permits arrive they must be admitted. Nevertheless it is extremely desirable that refugees arrive in small numbers whether by British or foreign vessels. When large numbers arrive by one boat whether for one port or several ports Press immediately gives prominence to the fact and strong representations for curtailment of issue of permits are made.[26]

In formulating its refugee policies, the government was far more concerned about domestic repercussions than about its international reputation. It did little to dispel the fear of many Australians that refugee immigrants would erode working conditions, live on the public purse or form ghettos in Australian cities; but it did not let the perceived mood of the electorate entirely dictate its actions.

CHAPTER 2

Balts

The government of Stanley Bruce was the first to embrace suggestions that Australia dramatically increase its population. In 1922, Bruce enthused: "Population is the golden key which will unlock all doors, sweep aside all obstacles."[1] He thought that an annual migrant intake in excess of 100,000 was both feasible and desirable. Bruce's ideas were not realised in the 1920s, falling victim to changing political and economic circumstances. Twenty years later, however, the fear of a Japanese invasion during the second world war had a lasting impact on the Australian government's attitude to immigration. The Curtin and Chifley governments became convinced that Australia's population needed to increase substantially to defend the country and expand its economy, and that immigration would play an important role in bringing about this growth. Still, it remained a long journey from this insight to the admission of more than 200,000 refugees in the first postwar decade.

In May 1945, Arthur Calwell, then Minister for Information and later one of the driving forces behind the push for a dramatic increase in Australia's migrant intake, published his thoughts about population policy in the booklet *How Many Australians Tomorrow?*. It was illustrated with numerous photographs of children, among them one of a blonde girl, which was captioned, "NEW AUSTRALIAN CITIZEN? A little Yugoslav refugee in a Middle East U.N.R.R.A. camp."[2] The booklet did not refer to refugee immigration. In fact, Calwell argued that Australia's main problem was its fertility rate rather than its immigration level. "Our first task is to ennoble motherhood," Calwell stated.[3]

He acknowledged that a rising fertility rate alone would not be sufficient to increase Australia's population dramatically. Yet the only non-British immigrants he seemed to have in mind were children (including, if the illustrations are any guide, refugee children). Calwell wrote:

> When we bring alien children here they can be more readily assimilated, will learn English and will absorb the Australian point of view more quickly than adults. The plan is to bring at least 17,000 children a year, and I hope the number will be increased to 50,000 a year.[4]

In July 1945, Calwell was appointed Australia's first Minister for Immigration. In August, he outlined his plans in parliament:

> If Australians have learned one lesson from the Pacific war now moving to a successful conclusion, it is surely that we cannot continue to hold our island continent for ourselves and our descendants unless we greatly increase our numbers.[5]

He argued for a 2 per cent annual increase in Australia's population, which numbered about 7.5 million at the time. He reiterated his conviction that higher birth rates ought to be the preferred solution, but said he would be prepared to agree to an annual migrant intake of 70,000 in times of a "fully-expanded economy." Calwell is sometimes credited with single-handedly initiating the mass immigration of non-British settlers. But at the time, the federal opposition was prepared to go further than Calwell. Responding to Calwell's statement on immigration policy, Robert Menzies said:

> We must be prepared to adopt an adventurous policy of migration. We must be prepared to take risks with some of our standards of perfection... in order to get people to come here... Let us bring to this country, not a few carefully handpicked people who, we think, are of our own kind. Whether they come from Europe, Great Britain or the United States, let us welcome all who have the vigour and enterprise to come here.[6]

By comparison, the Chifley government's approach was conservative, relying mainly on increasing the level of immigration from the British Isles.

By the end of 1946, the government realised its targets could not be met. Too few Britons responded to Australia's plea for more immigrants, and, more importantly, a severe shortage of shipping hampered the recruitment of settlers. But when, in early 1947, a senior official from the United Nations Relief and Rehabilitation Administration (UNRRA) urged Australia to resettle 30,000 refugees, Calwell rejected the proposal.[7]

Calwell's response to this and similar suggestions at this time has to be understood in the context of the public's response to the small-scale immigration of Jewish refugees in 1946 and early 1947. In 1945, he had authorised the granting of up to 2000 landing permits for Jewish refugees who had close relatives in Australia. Even before the first of them began arriving from East Asia and Europe in the second half of 1946, newspaper articles warned of a flood of Jewish immigrants. Once the first refugees had landed, representatives of returned servicemen's organisations and of the Australian Natives' Association drew on anti-Semitic stereotypes to protest loudly against their admission. The Association's chief president, P. J. Lynch, repeatedly suggested that the new arrivals represented the "refuse of Europe."[8]

In January 1947, in deference to the backlash against the admission of Jewish refugees, Calwell announced a change of policy:

> The Government feels that it has gone as far as it can reasonably be expected to go, for the present, in granting landing permits to persons of these classes on purely humanitarian grounds... It is intended that in future the approval of applications will depend more on the intending migrants' ability to contribute to Australia's economic welfare.[9]

Calwell also introduced a quota for ships carrying migrants to Australia: Jews were to comprise no more than 25 per cent of their passengers. In 1948, this rule was extended to planes.

It was the prime minister, Ben Chifley, rather than Calwell, who first realised that many of the refugees waiting for resettlement places in Europe were not Jewish. In mid 1947, Chifley authorised Calwell to travel to Europe to seek international assistance in obtaining shipping and to approach the recently formed International Refugee Organisation (IRO) about the possibility of recruiting migrants in European refugee camps.

The war, the Nazis' racial policies and Germany's insatiable demand for labour had resulted in the uprooting of millions of people. When the war in Europe ended, there were approximately 8.5 million displaced persons (DPs) in Germany alone, and another 2.5 million elsewhere in Europe. The Allied military authorities repatriated about seven million DPs within less than six months, and the UNRRA repatriated another million over the following eighteen months. But many DPs from Eastern Europe did not want to return home. It was these people who attracted the interest of Chifley and Calwell.

On 1 July 1947, the IRO took over the functions and activities of the UNRRA and the Intergovernmental Committee on Refugees. On 21 July, Australia agreed with the IRO to resettle 12,000 DPs per year over three years, and to contribute £12 per head for travel costs. On 28 November, the first 843 DPs arrived in Fremantle aboard a converted US warship, the *General Stuart Heintzelman.* About seven in every eight of the passengers were single men, with the remainder single women. All were originally from Estonia, Latvia or Lithuania.

Because these first "Balts" – as they were soon to be labelled – were received favourably by the Australian public, the government abandoned its cautious approach. In July 1948, Calwell announced that Australia would match a pledge by the United States government and "accept up to 200,000 people from the ranks of Europe's displaced persons if shipping can be obtained."[10] But in 1948, owing to the continuing shortage of shipping, only another 9000 IRO-sponsored refugees were moved to Australia.

In late 1948, the IRO secured more ships, and the number of DPs resettled in Australia increased dramatically. The 50,000th DP was due to arrive aboard the *Fairsea* in August 1949. The Department of Immigration decided to celebrate this milestone, and asked the Australian mission in Germany, which coordinated the Australian selection teams, to identify an "attractive female child under 10 accompanying parents who are suitable subject for publicity."[11] The authorities settled on Maira Kalnins, a girl who resembled the refugee child depicted in

How Many Australians Tomorrow?. According to Arthur Calwell's subsequent press statement, Maira was a "smiling, flaxen-haired girl of seven from Latvia, travelling with her five-year-old brother and her father and mother."[12] The Kalnins family had left their native Riga for Germany in 1944, fleeing the advancing Red Army. Maira's father had studied engineering and had a basic knowledge of English.

The Kalnins represented ideal non-British immigrants. At the time, they were also typical of the refugees admitted to Australia through the IRO, but not representative of the broader profile of DPs. In early 1948, an American ship's surgeon, Dr Ergas, accompanied another converted United States warship, the *General Black*, on two IRO-funded trips, the first from Naples to South America, and the second from the German port of Bremerhaven to Australia. About the first group of passengers, he wrote:

> Many of them had skin diseases... and some had venereal diseases. It was a blessing to them when they found out that we were so well equipped... to care for their various ailments... Men and women were a mixture of all ages and the majority of them had dark complexions, brown eyes and dark hair. Their past hardships hid much of their normal appearance. Many of them were melancoly [*sic*] with a sad, forced smile.[13]

All these people were resettled in either Venezuela or Peru. In February and March 1947, these countries had signed agreements with the Intergovernmental Committee on Refugees, and begun recruiting DPs in Europe – well before the Australians expressed interest in them. Most of the refugees resettled in Peru in the late 1940s were originally from Yugoslavia. The largest contingent of refugees accepted by Venezuela, which resettled 4250 refugees in 1947 alone, was from Poland.[14]

Ergas's description of the Australia-bound DPs suggests that they had little in common with those being resettled in Venezuela and Peru:

> Most of this group consisted of young men and women with very few children. They were well dressed, carried additional clothes, made a fine appearance, and looked bright and intelligent. Most of them were

from the Baltic countries... The majority spoke English and German... The women in general were very good looking. Some had beautiful, dark, long hair; others were platinum blonde with blue eyes, light complexion and very tall. The men were fine looking too. Many of these displaced persons had college and university degrees... All the immigrants had to pass a thorough physical examination by two Australian physicians before they were granted permission... to make the long journey to Australia. Anyone found with a lung or heart disease, or any other serious ailment, was rejected. It was indeed a very select group of young people. They all appeared to be energetic, ambitious, and full of life.[15]

The Australian government's decision in 1947 to admit a large number of DPs was motivated by its desire to significantly increase Australia's population – and, more specifically, its workforce – rather than by humanitarian considerations. Given that not enough suitable British settlers were available, Australia recruited other appropriate immigrants. Suitable non-British settlers were young, educated and healthy, and, ideally, possessed certain racial features. Australian selection teams preferred vigorous, flaxen-haired, fair-skinned and blue-eyed young men and women from the Baltic countries who did not want to or could not return to the Soviet Union. The government looked much less favourably on DPs from south-eastern Europe, not to mention survivors of German concentration camps who were ill as a result of their ordeal.

As the American doctor observed, Australian selection criteria were strict. In the late 1940s and early 1950s, Australia did not accept single men or married couples with children over the age of 45, or single women or childless married couples over the age of 40. Selection teams were instructed to recruit 60, and at times 70, workers per every 100 migrants. Operating Instruction No. 71 of 19 June 1950 informed selection teams:

Canberra has directed that "no family unit shall be eligible for selection where it comprises more persons than a man, wife and two children under 14 years of age."... [N]o group shall be accepted if it contains more than three dependants. As among dependants, wives and children are preferred... [N]ot more than one aged dependant is to be included in any family unit.[16]

At one stage, the Director-General of Health asked the medical officers selecting DPs in Europe to reject "cases requiring continued medical care even for minor complaints" – he had in mind bad teeth, varicose veins, tinea and other minor ailments – because he was concerned that the new settlers would otherwise be able to "utilise these disabilities to claim unfitness for work in particular localities or particular jobs."[17] The Australian immigration authorities accepted only one argument for a relaxation of their selection criteria: the selection teams' inability to meet recruitment targets and fill the available ships. As long as they could afford it, the selection teams adhered to the immigration department's "standards of perfection" and, to quote again Robert Menzies's reply to Calwell in August 1945, brought only "carefully handpicked people" to Australia – people who resembled Australia's "own kind" as closely as possible.

In 1949, refugees did not queue for a limited number of Australian resettlement places. Rather, the Australian immigration department – and its counterparts in Washington, Lima, Caracas and other New World capitals – queued for a limited number of ships ferrying DPs to their new homelands. Australian officials competed with the representatives of other resettlement countries: "the search for suitable settlers soon developed into a race between the major countries of immigration," Australia's pre-eminent authority on DP immigration, Egon Kunz, observed.[18] Government officials tried to sell Australia as a destination to the Kalnins and other potential immigrants from the Baltic countries in order to fill the IRO's ships with suitable settlers.

Over the course of 1948 and 1949, Calwell and his department became increasingly anxious not to miss out on a golden opportunity to people Australia at a very low cost. From initially wanting to admit non-British immigrants only as children, to then asking his selection teams to recruit only DPs from the Baltic states, Calwell had come a long way. In April 1950, a few months after the Labor government had been voted out of office, he admonished his successor, Harold Holt: "I think that we should get all who are available of those good people, and get them while we can, because next year will be too late."[19] He was afraid it would be too late for Australia if its government allowed the "good people" to be resettled in the Americas. Successive Ministers for Immigration and their departments did not press for the resettlement of refugees because they were concerned for refugees languishing in camps in countries of first asylum.

More than 180,000 people were resettled in Australia under the auspices of the IRO, which was disbanded in 1953. They represented more than half of all immigrants in the period 1948 to 1953, and more than a quarter of Australia's overall humanitarian intake since the second world war. Never again would Australia admit such a large number of refugees per year, and in proportion to its overall migrant intake, as in the late 1940s and early 1950s. By comparison, New Zealand admitted fewer than 5000 IRO-sponsored migrants. The IRO's role in sponsoring the immigration of European refugees to Australia was taken over by the Intergovernmental Committee for European Migration, which up to 1973, according to Charles Price, facilitated the movement of 628,000 migrants to Australia, among them 199,000 refugees.[20]

Between 1947 and 1956, most refugees resettled in Australia were Eastern Europeans who were in Germany or Austria at the end of the second world war and did not want to return to the Soviet Union or Poland. There were also Eastern European "escapees" who had fled to West Germany, Italy, Austria or other parts of Western Europe after their countries had fallen to the communists in the immediate postwar years. By far the largest refugee exodus at the time – ethnic Germans forced to leave former German territories in Poland, Czechoslovakia and the Soviet Union – made no impact outside of Germany, where the *Heimatvertriebene* (expellees) were resettled. But other than the steady trickle of people leaving Eastern Europe, there were no large-scale refugee movements in Europe in the first half of the 1950s: most of those classified as refugees in the mid 1950s had been outside their home countries for several years.

In 1956, this trickle temporarily became a stream. On 23 October, several hundred thousand Hungarians demonstrating in the streets of Budapest clashed with local and Soviet troops. On 1 November, Prime Minister Imre Nagy, who led a reformist government, proposed the withdrawal of his country from the Warsaw Pact. Three days later, the

Soviet army attacked Budapest, crushed popular resistance and installed a conformist government. Over the ensuing months, some 180,000 Hungarians fled across the border to Austria, and another 20,000 to Yugoslavia. Austria was not able to deal with the influx, and on 5 November appealed to the United Nations High Commissioner for Refugees (UNHCR) for help.

Australia was quick to react. On 8 November, the Minister for Immigration, Athol Townley, announced in parliament that for the remainder of the financial year Australia was going to provide sanctuary for up to 3000 refugees from Hungary who had fled to Austria.[21] Four weeks later, the government increased the figure to 5000. Compared with its response to those fleeing Nazi Germany during the second half of the 1930s, Australia's reaction was swift and generous. So was that of other Western countries; at the height of the Cold War, anti-communist refugees had a high propaganda value. In fact, compared with the commitments made by other countries, Australia's response was rather modest.

The diplomat Gordon Jockel was arguing the Hungarians' case from Geneva, where he represented Australia at the UNHCR. "Position thus is that Australia undertook to take 3,000 refugees when total was 20,000 and we are now intending to limit our intake to 5,000 although the total has risen to 140,000," he told his superiors in Canberra in December 1956.[22] He also pointed out that his government expected other countries to fund Australia's resettlement of Hungarian refugees, and that the acceptance of 5000 refugees was merely covering the expected shortfall in the annual migrant intake:

> As regards the five thousand refugees we have already decided to take we are contributing $85 per capita to transport costs representing our normal proportion of the costs of each migrant moved by I.C.E.M. to Australia. The gap of $65 we are presumably intending to leave I.C.E.M. to fill out of its general resources and special appeals. (In this connection our contribution of £A.10,000 to I.C.E.M.'s appeal for the Hungarian programme would close this gap for about 370 movements only to Australia.) In my view this is not good enough especially if our action is being taken within our ordinary migration framework.

Jockel was in constant contact with people working for the United Nations and with other diplomats in Geneva. He was acutely aware of factors influencing Australia's reputation overseas:

> We have to consider our general position internationally as one of the two or three major immigration countries... [W]e are so far only taking a volume of Hungarian refugees sufficient to meet the shortfall in our regular migration intake, at little or no cost to ourselves beyond our contribution for normal migrants, and at added costs to other I.C.E.M. contributors.[23]

Whether it was because Jockel's arguments were convincing, or because Australia did not want to forego an opportunity of recruiting suitable migrants, on 22 January 1957, Townley committed Australia to resettling an additional 5000 refugees.[24] By 1959, 14,000 Hungarians had arrived in Australia.

Australia also resettled about 6000 Czechs and Slovaks after the suppression of the Prague Spring, which had flourished under the reformist government of Alexander Dubček. This represented about 2.5 per cent of those who fled when the armies of five Warsaw Pact nations invaded Czechoslovakia in August 1968.

•

In numerical terms, Australia's postwar resettlement effort was most impressive. Only the United States admitted more refugees for resettlement than Australia during the first thirty years after the war. Between 1945 and 1966, New Zealand admitted only 6934 refugees sponsored by the Intergovernmental Committee on Refugees, the United Nations Relief and Rehabilitation Administration, the IRO or the Intergovernmental Committee for European Migration. Over the same period, Australia resettled more than 40 times that many people in the same category.[25]

But to appreciate the nature of Australia's refugee resettlement programme in the first fifteen years after the second world war, when Australia accepted 250,000 refugees, it is necessary to ask whom Australia did not accept. In the next chapter, I discuss the admission (or non-admission) of non-European refugees. But not all Europeans were welcome either. Much as the current immigration department highlights Australia's offshore humanitarian intake, in the late 1950s the department stressed Australia's contribution to the resettlement of European DPs. In 1957, for example, the department's secretary, Tasman Heyes, boasted in a personal letter to George Warren of the United States State Department:

> We have, of course, been perhaps the largest recipient, apart from your own country, of refugees since the war. We accepted more than 200,000 displaced persons; we were the principal country recruiting refugees in Trieste; we are currently recruiting 15,000 Hungarians, of whom approximately two-thirds have already arrived; we are on the point of commencing our recruitment of Hungarians in Yugoslavia, and as a normal procedure we accept up to 5% of our recruitment in all European countries from amongst refugee groups in those countries.[26]

In a similar vein two years later, a lengthy document on Australia's postwar resettlement programme prepared by the Department of Immigration proudly asserted: "In proportion to its population Australia has led the world in accepting refugees for resettlement."[27] It is indicative of Australia's approach that Heyes and his department used the verbs "to accept" (signalling altruism) and "to recruit" (signalling self-interest) synonymously.

The department's claims about Australia's record in resettling refugees, both now and in 1959, are undoubtedly correct. By emphasising this record now, the department wants to divert attention from Australia's treatment of onshore asylum seekers. In the late 1950s, it was concerned to protect Australia from questions about its record in dealing with what was often termed either the "residual refugee problem" or the "hard core."

The "hard core" were refugees according to the 1951 Refugee Convention (that is, as a result of events occurring before 1 January 1951 in Europe) who could not be resettled. Some of them, including thousands of White Russians, were stranded in China, Hong Kong and Korea. In the late 1950s and early 1960s, Australia admitted thousands of White Russian refugees from China and Manchuria; between 1963 and 1965, it granted visas to about 2500 Armenians from Syria and

Egypt.[28] In the late 1950s, most refugees belonging to the "hard core" were, however, in Europe. By late 1959, some 25,000 refugees were still living in official camps in Austria, Italy and Greece. For the majority of them, resettlement countries could not be found because they were old, disabled, chronically ill, or single mothers, often referred to as "socially handicapped cases."

Until 1959, no resettlement country accepted families in which one or more members had a disability. In a major breakthrough in February 1959, the New Zealand government decided to accept twenty such families for resettlement. The High Commissioner for Refugees, Auguste Lindt, praised this "magnanimous gesture" and correctly predicted that it would have "a powerful impact on other countries of resettlement."[29] A few months later, the Australian government followed the New Zealand lead. Charles Price remembers the occasion in his account of Australian refugee policies:

> In July 1959 Alex Downer [affirmed] the government's strong commitment to solving the hard-core problem and [announced] that Australia had decided to make a special gesture and take responsibility for – and here we all sat forward on our seats expecting to hear a figure of at least 500 – "no less than 20 handicapped families."[30]

Later, the government, perhaps to better the performance of its neighbour across the Tasman, raised that figure to 200. It also allowed for the immigration of another 300 such families provided they were sponsored and would be cared for by non-government organisations.

These concessions occurred against the backdrop of World Refugee Year in 1959–60, a highly successful private initiative which gained the backing of the UNHCR and of many governments, including Australia's. World Refugee Year generated unprecedented public awareness about refugee issues in the Australian community, and gave government and non-government organisations an opportunity to lobby the public on behalf of refugees. The Australian government's admission of a comparatively large number of refugees with a disability was a sign that the public had responded well to lobbying.

Commenting on the success of World Refugee Year in New Zealand, its prime minister, Walter Nash, observed: "The extent to which any country can receive refugees depends upon the goodwill and assistance which the residents of that country are prepared to offer."[31] Nash's observation remains largely true for refugees admitted for humanitarian reasons. As World Refugee Year showed, collective goodwill could be generated and nurtured. During the period discussed in this book, World Refugee Year was the only occasion when the Australian government supported a concerted public campaign designed to garner support for the admission of refugees.

In early 1960, the High Commissioner for Refugees suggested that the Australian authorities publicise the arrival of the 250,000th refugee as part of World Refugee Year activities. The Department of Immigration welcomed the idea. It decided to delay the event to make it coincide with an appeal for World Refugee Year, and to select a refugee with a physical handicap to emphasise Australia's contribution to resettling the "hard core."[32] But the selection of a suitable person proved complicated. The first two candidates were Poles who had had tuberculosis. One of them had contracted the disease in a German concentration camp and had long since been cured. Neither of them was acceptable to the department because it was not prepared to admit tuberculosis cases above its quota of thirteen.[33] Three further candidates were also rejected – in one case apparently because the applicant had lost a leg after the war rather than as a direct result of the war.

The department finally selected Otto Kampe, a 41-year-old Latvian, who could walk only with the help of crutches because he had suffered from bilateral hip disease as a child. It says much about the department's confidence in its selection process that it was not afraid that the publicity surrounding Kampe's arrival would highlight his previous failed attempts to immigrate. Kampe was a well-qualified designer. His physical disability did not affect his capacity to work in his profession. His sisters and his mother had migrated to Australia in 1950 and 1951, respectively. For ten years, Kampe had tried to follow them. Yet it was only when the department was looking for an attractive family to publicise Australia's acceptance of disabled refugees as part of World Refugee Year that his application to join his family was finally successful.

Kampe was accompanied by his wife and five children. In a press statement announcing their arrival, the Minister for Immigration,

Alexander Downer, made much of the fact that Australia had not simply accepted a "permanent cripple," but had gained seven settlers who would benefit Australia:

> In accepting the Kampe family we will gain not only five fine, healthy young future Australians, but two courageous people who have shown by their fortitude and their strength of character in the most unfortunate circumstances that they will make truly worthy citizens.[34]

When welcoming the Kampes at Essendon Airport, Downer again stressed the contribution Australia expected from them. The *Sun* reported:

> "You are an artist and a designer," said Mr Downer, in a clear, ringing tone. "You are going to be important to Australia and we can do with many more people of your type."[35]

Perhaps buoyed by Australia's contribution to World Refugee Year – which included a concession on the age limits for refugees as well as the acceptance of 180 families from the "hard core" – in June 1960, the High Commissioner wrote to the Department of Immigration seeking its help in solving refugee problems outside Austria, Germany, Italy and Greece, where Australia recruited UNHCR-sponsored refugees. Lindt asked Australia to extend the assisted passage scheme to Albanian and Bulgarian refugees in Yugoslavia, Bulgarians in Turkey, and Spaniards, Russians, Poles and Czechs in Morocco.[36] The department's reply once again made it clear that Australia was not guided by the plight of individual refugees but by the prospect of gaining suitable settlers: "Our limited knowledge of the refugee potential in [Yugoslavia, Turkey and Morocco] does not lead us to believe that they would be suitable areas for special recruitment." The department was only willing to reconsider its stance if the High Commissioner could demonstrate "that there are suitable settlers amongst the refugee population in these countries."[37]

How generous was Australia in response to Europe's postwar refugee crises? The size of Australia's refugee intake has to be seen in the context of the government's motivation for resettling Eastern European DPs, Hungarians, Czechs and Slovaks, and White Russians.

Before 1960, assisted refugee migration to Australia was almost totally divorced from humanitarian motives, and thus from the needs of individual refugees. In contrast, New Zealand's overall resettlement record was negligible, while it took in a comparatively large number of refugees for humanitarian reasons.

In the days of the DP resettlement programme, the Australian authorities did not even want to draw on the humanitarian argument for tactical reasons. In early 1949, the immigration publicity officer of the Department of Information pointed out:

> It was never our intention to find acceptance for the displaced persons through an appeal to the charity and sympathy of the Australian people. An acceptance born of these sentiments can turn easily to... contempt. The line we took was one of frank reporting of facts. We pulled no punches and we made no apologies. We stated frankly the terms of the agreement under which the displaced persons entered Australia (for two years to be under Commonwealth direction)... Such a frank line appealed to the Australian people.[38]

Australian refugee policy was guided by humanitarian considerations only in relation to unassisted refugee migration in the immediate postwar period. But then Australia's decision to admit a limited number of Jewish survivors was curtailed by fears of being swamped by Jewish refugees, the same fears that had informed government policies in the late 1930s.

CHAPTER 3

Ineligibles

The 1956 Hungarian uprising and the suppression of the Prague Spring were only two of the political developments producing mass refugee movements in the 1950s, 1960s and early 1970s. Between 1949 and 1951 alone, in the immediate aftermath of the establishment of the People's Republic of China, some 700,000 of its citizens sought refuge in Hong Kong. Chinese refugees continued to arrive there throughout the 1950s and 1960s. In the second half of the 1950s, during the Algerian civil war, several hundred thousand people fled to Tunisia and Morocco. In 1961, a Hutu-led *coup d'état* in Rwanda led to the displacement of about 120,000 Tutsi. By 1965, there were 850,000 refugees in Africa alone.[1]

In the 1950s and 1960s, Asian or African refugees were rarely offered permanent resettlement outside Asia or Africa. Australia, for one, was not prepared to accommodate Chinese, Algerian or Rwandan refugees. As long as the White Australia policy determined its approach to immigration, Australia resettled only refugees who met its requirements about colour, race and upbringing. Between 1950 and 1957, for instance, immigrants had to be "European rather than non-European in appearance," "75% or more of European descent," and "fully European in upbringing and outlook."[2]

From the 1950s onwards, the Australian government became increasingly aware that its immigration policy was difficult to defend overseas. It feared it might be either pressured into accepting non-European refugees or ostracised if it successfully resisted international pressure. In the late 1950s and early 1960s, the government was particularly concerned about the prospect of having to respond to the refugee crisis in Hong Kong. For a long time it tried to hide behind the argument that the Chinese fleeing to Hong Kong were not refugees in the strict sense. It therefore resisted the involvement of the United Nations High Commissioner for Refugees (UNHCR), as I discuss in more detail in Chapter 6. The matter was complicated by Cold War politics. And given that Hong Kong was a British colony, Australia also did not want to appear unsympathetic about the problems faced by the Hong Kong and British administrations. The Australian government was concerned, too, that an unsympathetic stance would focus undue international attention on its restricted immigration policy.

In the postwar period, those administering Australia's foreign affairs tended to view the White Australia policy as a liability, and tried to keep it out of the international limelight. In 1957, the diplomat Ralph Harry, who had served as Australia's representative in Geneva, noted with alarm that Hong Kong's governor had contrasted the UNHCR's involvement in resettling Hungarian refugees with its lack of action on Chinese refugees. Harry told a high-level contact in the Hong Kong government that "statements like these might well focus international attention on Australian policy and that [the Hong Kong government] should give some consideration to this when determining their own policy."[3]

Australia was also concerned when its rigid stance was exposed by countries that traditionally pursued very similar policies. In 1962, for example, it was once more New Zealand that appeared to upstage Australia, when the government in Wellington announced it would admit twenty Chinese orphans from Hong Kong for resettlement.[4] In this case, however, the token gesture arguably backfired when a visiting UNHCR representative told New Zealanders that the offer had been a "mistaken effort" because "adopted children usually grew up much happier and better adjusted if their foster parents were of the same race and background."[5] Australian diplomats, who closely followed the case, would have been grateful for the unexpected support from the UNHCR.

For the period from 1945 to 1965, I could find no exceptions to Australia's refusal to admit non-European refugees. In 1966, the government gave in to domestic and international pressure and created a new visa category for non-Europeans with special skills. The policy provided that non-European applicants could be exempted from the usual racial requirements if they were "[p]ersons with specialized technical skills for appointments for which local residents are not available."[6] The following year, the UNHCR asked Australia to accept 36 Chinese Sisters of the Franciscan Missionaries of Mary from Macao. Commenting on his negotiations with the UNHCR, the immigration department's assistant secretary, Ted Charles, noted that the Sisters:

> have already experienced rough handling by the Chinese (especially their members who were in mainland China). I said that we would consider sympathetically any request received. I did not see their entry as posing any problem from the policy viewpoint... [I]t would be in line with the Minister's recent expression of view on the entry of non-Europeans as members of religious Orders in Australia. The refugee aspect of the situation would also be relevant.[7]

But this was an exceptional case. It involved a small number of women persecuted for their Christian – and, presumably, anti-communist – beliefs, who were unlikely to sponsor family members to follow them to Australia, and who would not bear children. Even then, Charles agreed to the women's admission primarily on the grounds that it did not contravene established immigration policy rather than because they could be regarded as refugees.

While generally trying to stay clear of resettlement schemes for non-European refugees, the Australian government was willing to help out in cases where Europeans living in non-European countries were afraid of losing their privileges and were looking for a new home. In the immediate postwar period, as the former British and Dutch colonial empires in Asia crumbled, Australia became the preferred destination of many Europeans living in South and Southeast Asia. And in the early 1960s, Australia expected British settlers in southern and East Africa to constitute a new pool of potential immigrants, as political unrest deepened in South Africa, and decolonisation proceeded rapidly elsewhere in the continent. Thus in April 1962, a Liberal New South Wales senator, John McCallum, asked in question time:

> Having in mind the present disturbed state of parts of Africa and the probability that a good many Africans of European descent will be looking for security elsewhere, particularly for their children, are any new steps being taken by the Department of Immigration to obtain desirable migrants for Australia from those sources?[8]

Australia could not openly invite applications from South Africans because it did not want to be accused of poaching settlers from another Commonwealth country. But many Europeans leaving southern and East Africa in the early 1960s were British nationals. They did not need to apply for a visa to Australia and often even had access to assisted passages. They were welcome not so much because of the circumstances that occasioned their departure from Africa, but rather because of their suitability as immigrants. A couple of days after McCallum's question in the Senate, the head of the immigration department, Peter Heydon, received two visitors who were exploring Australia's potential "as a refuge for Europeans from Kenya," which was approaching independence. In his diary, Heydon noted:

> In these matters we cannot advertise or publicise but in a quiet way we are trying to make sure that shipping is available and that applications are handled properly because while I think I will be opposed to having tens of thousands of these people, a few thousands [*sic*] of them should integrate well and be a useful supplement to what we call the intake.[9]

Australia's attitude to Europeans emigrating from East Africa in the early 1960s contrasted sharply not only with its approach to Chinese refugees in Hong Kong seeking resettlement at the same time, but also with its subsequent response to non-European refugees in Africa. Eight years after Kenya's imminent independence made Australia an attractive migration option for the country's European population, the Kenyan government told the country's Asian community (who were mainly from the Indian subcontinent) that they were no longer welcome unless they had taken out Kenyan citizenship at the time of independence. Kenya then had an Asian population of close to 200,000, more than half of whom were non-citizens.

In 1970, the idea of resettling a contingent of non-European refugees in Australia did not seem as far-fetched as it had ten years earlier. Since the immigration reforms of 1966, more than 10,000 non-Europeans had migrated to Australia. In an editorial, the *Australian* called for a Kenyan refugee resettlement scheme – if only to "offset some of the growing criticism of Australian racialism."[10] But the government was unwilling to countenance such a scheme. When the media reported that the New Settlers Federation was encouraging Kenya's Indians to move to Australia, Cabinet reacted with alarm. On 30 April 1970, it "was agreed as to the need for prompt action to forestall this attempt by the New Settlers Federation to force an issue on Australia's immigration policy."[11]

The anticipated pressure on Australia's immigration policy did not, however, eventuate. The Kenyan government did not expel longtime residents of Asian origin, and most of those who chose to leave went to the United Kingdom. Some, though, tried to migrate to Australia under its existing immigration policy. The application in 1970 of Geraldine R., a 23-year-old shorthand typist of Goanese ancestry, was a litmus test of the government's willingness to admit qualified applicants among Kenya's Asians. According to the Australian immigration attaché in Nairobi, R. was:

> western in dress, of R[oman] C[atholic] religion, and European in manner and outlook. She has a bright cheerful nature and speaks English fluently without the usual Indian accent. I consider that she would integrate readily into the Australian community.[12]

There were other aspects of her application that counted in her favour: she was joint holder of the East African record for shorthand; her employers had offered her a position in their Sydney branch office; and none of her relatives wanted to accompany her to Australia. While Geraldine R.'s qualifications and skills were below those envisaged when the 1966 reforms were introduced, the Minister for Immigration had in previous years approved applications by single female applicants with lesser qualifications "in the interests of obtaining a balance of the sexes." But in this case, the government rejected the application so as not to encourage Kenya's Asians to turn to Australia. The departmental submission to the minister argued: "If we ease requirements for one Asian in East Africa we could very easily create a difficult precedent which could be used by many others." The Minister for Immigration, Phillip Lynch, agreed.[13]

The imaginary floodgates remained closed. While there was, in the end, no deluge of applications from Kenya's non-indigenous minorities, pressure to accept non-European refugees from Africa suddenly built up again in 1972. This time, the crisis was not merely imaginary. In early August, Uganda's president, Idi Amin, who had seized power in a military coup eighteen months earlier, decreed that all non-citizens of South Asian ancestry had to leave the country within 90 days. Between August and November, more than 50,000 Asians, including many who had taken out Ugandan citizenship in 1962, were forced to flee. Britain resettled more than half of them. Canada accepted some 6000 expellees and India 10,000.

Australia's response was comparatively miserly. Some ten days after Amin's announcement, the Minister for Immigration, Jim Forbes, told parliament he did not expect to be approached by Britain about the resettlement of Uganda's Asians, and asserted his government's "firm and unshakeable determination... to maintain a homogeneous society in Australia."[14] But the British government, unable to cope with the Ugandan crisis on its own, did request Australia's help. On 29 August, the Foreign and Commonwealth Office in London submitted an annotated list of potential resettlement countries to the British prime minister. The entry under "Australia" includes the following observations:

> The Cabinet have decided that they cannot depart from their normal immigration policy ie to take only professionally qualified immigrants. It appears that Ministers are unwilling to risk forfeiting votes in the forthcoming elections.[15]

Australia's high commissioner in London, Alexander Downer (the former Minister for Immigration), had strongly supported the British government's appeal for help. He suggested that Australia offer to admit in the order of 2000 expellees. Downer's argument was similar to that made by Bruce in 1938 for the admission of refugees from Nazi

Germany. Like Bruce, Downer believed that Australia's reputation was at stake.[16] Responding to a letter from an Australian living in London, who had told him that it "becomes increasingly difficult to be proud of Australia,"[17] Downer distinguished clearly between his own view and that of the government he represented: "The Australian government should be prepared, on the grounds of humanity, to accept some of these unfortunate people, and incidentally help the British government over a very difficult – and unfair – stile."[18]

In 1972, Australia's immigration policy no longer enjoyed bipartisan support. The Labor Party attacked the government's restricted immigration policy – and abolished it the following year, having been elected in late 1972. But Jim Forbes could count on support from the former leader of the opposition, Arthur Calwell. Calwell was certain that "the overwhelming majority of Australians do not want to see any Ugandan Asians brought to Australia" and was afraid the government would let in Ugandan refugees on humanitarian grounds alone.[19] Calwell need not have worried. By 6 October 1972, one month before the expiry of Amin's deadline, Australia had approved a mere 71 applications covering 198 people. Of these, 173 were approved under the existing non-European policy "on the basis of qualifications held by the principal applicant," and the remainder on the basis of family sponsorship.[20]

The immigration department applied the non-European policy scrupulously to Asian applicants from Uganda. On 27 September 1972, the immigration attaché sent to Kampala to interview applicants was advised:

> Applications by engineers in all branches of engineering with exception of civil, heating and ventilation, instrumentation and refrigeration may be rejected without reference unless special circumstances apart from conditions in Uganda exist.[21]

On 2 December, the Labor Party won the federal election, and Gough Whitlam formed a government. Labor was committed to abolishing the last vestiges of the White Australia policy; but the government's approach to the Ugandan refugee crisis did not change much. In late October, the UNHCR had arranged for the emergency evacuation of all Ugandan Asians who had not yet found a country of asylum. Some 3600 refugees were flown to transit camps in Belgium, Italy, Malta, Austria and Spain. On 21 December, Whitlam announced that Australia was contributing an additional US$75,000 to assist the UNHCR in its work with Asians from Uganda. But he made no mention of Australian resettlement places.[22] When Whitlam was asked during a visit to London in April 1973 whether the abolition of the White Australia policy meant Australia would accommodate more Asians from Uganda, he replied: "If they have got qualifications such as entitle people to come to Australia then certainly they can come."[23] This was essentially the same answer as that given by the Minister for Immigration in the previous government: refugees were welcome as long as they qualified as immigrants. The Whitlam government did agree, however, to a UNHCR request to issue an additional 50 visas for Asian refugees from Uganda living in European transit camps.[24]

•

Before 1966, the White Australia policy barred non-European refugees from entering Australia; non-European refugees trying to enter between 1966 and 1973 fared only marginally better. But the government's understanding of who qualified as European, and who did not, changed. For example, in 1947, the Chifley government introduced a quota for Jewish immigrants, which limited the number of Jewish survivors able to migrate to Australia (see Chapter 2). It obviously considered Jews to be distinct from Europeans. The Menzies government abolished that quota but, during the 1950s, continued to oppose the immigration of Sephardic Jews and Jews of Middle East origin on the basis that they were not predominantly European.[25] But in 1969, the Gorton government raised no such objections when Australia was asked to admit Iraqi Jews persecuted by the Ba'athist regime.[26]

On one occasion, the government changed Australia's restricted immigration policy to accommodate immigrants who, while not refugees in the sense of the 1951 Refugee Convention, came to Australia to escape discrimination in their own country. The White Australia policy allowed for the immigration of people of "mixed descent." From 1957, Australia required of immigrants that "their appearance must be such as to satisfy the officer that they are of 75%

or more European descent and that they will have no difficulty in being accepted as Europeans in Australia."[27] Prospective immigrants affected by the 75 per cent rule included Southern Europeans such as Sicilians and Greeks, but the largest group of "mixed descent" immigrants in the late 1950s and early 1960s came from South Asia: they included Ceylonese Burghers, Anglo-Indians, Anglo-Burmese and Anglo-Pakistanis.

From the immigration department's point of view, these people – whose ancestors included Dutch and Sinhalese, or English and Bengali – were desirable immigrants. They spoke English at home, identified as Europeans and as white, were British nationals, tended to be well-educated, and assimilated easily. But many of them did not meet the department's requirements in terms of race and, even more so, skin colour. The Australian high commissioner in Colombo once explained that even applicants with a predominantly European ancestry tended to be too dark because "the Sinhalese who are themselves racially allied to the peoples of South India are a particularly dark people."[28]

The early 1960s saw a dramatic increase in the number of applications from Burghers and Anglo-Burmese, partly because of the Ceylonese and Burmese governments' discriminatory policies and the increasing marginalisation of Europeans of mixed descent in Ceylon and Burma. In 1964, the immigration department lobbied for a number of changes to the White Australia policy, including changes to the "mixed descent" policy. The changes were to allow the minister to admit applicants on the grounds that they were suffering discrimination, and were designed to make it possible for Ceylonese Burghers and Anglo-Burmese in particular to immigrate even if they did not meet the requirements of the 75 per cent rule.

In September 1964, while rejecting the department's proposed wide-ranging reforms of the White Australia policy (which were strongly supported by its minister, Hubert Opperman), Cabinet authorised the Minister for Immigration

> to admit for permanent residence persons of mixed-race where... humanitarian considerations, involving close family relationship or hardship on grounds of discrimination, are present... if the applicant shows by appearance, education, upbringing, outlook, mode of dress

> and way of living, that he is capable of ready integration into the Australian community.[29]

Perhaps aware of the significance of these amendments, and of their potential to erode the White Australia policy, Cabinet decided that "these changes should be made administratively, i.e. without public announcement."[30] When implementing the Cabinet decision of September 1964, the Department of Immigration tended to pay close attention to evidence of family ties in Australia, with few applicants admitted on the grounds of discrimination.[31] Thus departmental practice ran counter to the new policy's initial intention.

The idea that humanitarian considerations – other than the evidence of close family ties in Australia – should influence the outcome of applications was perhaps too novel a concept to make sense to many of the department's officers.

To the Department of Immigration, it did not matter whether push or pull factors motivated prospective immigrants, as long as it could select Australia's intake from a suitably large pool. During the period covered in this book, British migrants comprised by far the largest contingent selected from this pool. Before 1947 and between 1961 and 1973, the majority of those migrating to Australia were from the British Isles. In the 1960s, Ceylonese Burghers who identified as white and South Africans of European extraction were considered a "useful supplement" to the predominantly Anglo-Celtic intake. Chinese refugees fleeing to Hong Kong in the late 1950s and early 1960s, and Asians expelled from Uganda in 1972, were not. That they – unlike prospective immigrants from Britain, Germany, Holland, Italy and Greece – urgently needed to find a country willing to take them in had no bearing on the policy that determined the intake's composition.

CHAPTER 4

Asylum seekers

In September 1969, the Labor Party's Jim Mulvihill enquired in the Senate about how many people had been granted political asylum in Australia in the past five years.[1] After obtaining departmental advice, Senator Annabel Rankin, speaking on behalf of the Minister for Immigration, replied: "None."[2] In its briefing, the department had gone further, claiming that Vladimir Petrov, the Soviet diplomat who had defected in 1954, had in fact been the "last person accorded political asylum in Australia."[3] Not least because of the long-term consequences his request for political asylum had on the Australian political scene, his action had become part of the Australian vocabulary: to seek political asylum was to "do a Petrov."[4] How correct was the department's advice? Was Petrov really the only one to have "done a Petrov" in Australia? And if the advice were correct, did it reflect either the infrequency of requests for political asylum or else the government's hard-hearted response to such requests during the 1950s and 1960s?

Vladimir Petrov, Third Secretary of the Soviet embassy in Canberra, formally sought political asylum on 2 April 1954. On 20 April his wife, Evdokia Petrova, also requested political asylum. Or rather, Australian Security Intelligence Organisation (ASIO) officers (in the case of Petrov) and the Acting Administrator of the Northern Territory (in the case of Petrova) repeatedly offered political asylum to the two Soviet citizens, and, when these offers were finally accepted, produced applications ready for their signature. Petrova actually refused to sign this application; in her case, as the Acting Administrator later recalled, her "orally expressed wish was sufficient for our purposes."[5]

The Australian authorities were interested in Petrov because they believed he possessed material that would uncover a Soviet spy ring in Australia. In return for his cooperation, Australia was willing to offer political asylum, financial support and protection from his former masters. When ASIO first approached senior government officers about Petrov's impending defection, the solicitor-general, Kenneth Bailey, suggested that asylum should not simply be offered to Petrov to "save his skin," but, given the likely "high diplomatic and political repercussions," only "for something we get out of it," namely valuable intelligence.[6] ASIO agreed.

Petrova's case was different: ASIO did not expect her to have any intelligence value. On the evening of 19 April, two armed Soviet diplomatic couriers escorted her on board a Darwin-bound plane at Sydney's Mascot Airport. From Darwin, she was to continue to Moscow via Singapore. Angry anti-communist demonstrators converged on the plane. Petrova was held tightly by her escorts and was clearly distressed. In his book on the Petrov affair, Robert Manne describes how the Australian public came to remember the event:

> The nation saw an attractive young blonde woman, weeping and vulnerable, one foot bare, being dragged across the tarmac by two formidable, scowling Slavic gorillas. A durable visual image of what most Australians still believed the Cold War to be about – the struggle between the forces of Evil and Good – penetrated the national consciousness.[7]

That same evening, anti-communist crusader and member of the House of Representatives, Bill Wentworth, who was among the crowd at Mascot, conveyed his own impression of the events to Menzies and his Cabinet colleagues. He implored them to ensure that Petrova was given the opportunity to defect at Darwin unless they wanted to ruin the government's chance of winning the next election. It was only then that the government instructed the Northern Territory's Acting Administrator to approach Petrova.

At the time of Vladimir and Evdokia Petrov's defection, Australia did not have an asylum seeker policy. Nor was its government able to draw on a body of international law that prescribed its and the Petrovs' rights and obligations. The Petrovs were the first to formally seek and be granted political asylum in Australia. As I discuss in Chapters 1 and 2, Australia accepted some 10,000 refugees in the late 1930s and resettled about 200,000 displaced persons (DPs) in the first post-war decade. All those arriving as refugees or DPs were authorised to enter Australia. They usually held landing permits and were permitted to remain in the Commonwealth. They are thus not comparable with those we now call asylum seekers: non-citizens who are admitted to Australia temporarily as tourists or students (or diplomats, as in Petrov's case) and who apply for political asylum some time after having legally entered the country; or refugees who enter Australia without a valid visa and ask for asylum after they have been intercepted by border security agencies.

But even before 1954, refugees sometimes entered Australia either under false pretences, as tourists, or without applying for any kind of visa, by jumping ship or as stowaways. During the late 1930s, for instance, several German merchant seamen jumped ship in Australia because they had experienced or feared persecution in Germany. Instead of asking for political asylum, they evaded the Australian authorities as long as they could. Once they were found, the authorities could administer the dictation test, have them convicted as prohibited immigrants, and arrange for their deportation after release from prison. But they were usually allowed to remain in Australia. To the Department of the Interior, which was then responsible for immigration control, it did not matter why they had left Germany. Their motivation became an issue only after the outbreak of the second world war, when they became enemy aliens on account of their nationality and were faced with the prospect of internment.

George Huelscher, one such deserter, was fourteen when the Nazis came to power. From a young age, he worked as a sailor on ships plying Germany's rivers and canals. A few years later he recalled:

> I worked at different towns along the river, and I saw how things were going, and I was definitely anti-Nazi because I saw the way they were

> ruling. You were put into concentration camps and children never saw their mothers again... No one could believe it, but I dared not say anything aginst [*sic*] it.[8]

In 1937, he made a remark that was taken to be critical of the regime. He was arrested by the Gestapo, but released with a warning.

After his release, Huelscher worked on ocean-going ships. Together with a friend he jumped ship at Newcastle in December 1938. Neither Customs nor the Department of the Interior were initially willing to press charges against Huelscher (who could easily have been deported as a prohibited immigrant). It was only on 1 September 1939, the first day of the war, that Huelscher was arrested in Maitland. A few days later, he was discharged, after the police offered "no evidence as the Customs Dept. & Dept. of Interior did not wish any action."[9] Like nearly all of the German ship-jumpers in the second half of the 1930s, Huelscher was young, single, male, healthy and non-Jewish. He was welcome as an immigrant – and in that sense it did not matter at all why he chose to come to Australia. In a directive issued in 1936, the Department of the Interior advised that the Collector of Customs was not obliged to charge a "deserter of good type" with being a prohibited immigrant, and that if such charges were laid, it was not always desirable to secure an immediate conviction.[10]

Also in the late 1930s, some Jewish refugees entered Australia as tourists. The Department of the Interior made shipping companies responsible for ensuring that only bona fide visitors (which the shipping lines correctly interpreted to mean non-Jewish tourists) or refugees with landing permits were embarked for Australian ports. But those German Jews who arrived surreptitiously on round-the-world tickets were not usually deported. Australia applied its immigration regulations flexibly: as long as these refugees complied with the White Australia policy they were treated much like other prospective immigrants.

In another instance, on 10 August 1941, a stowaway was discovered among a group of Polish refugees who had reached Sydney on the *Kasima Maru* from Japan (see Chapter 1). He was Hersz Rozenberg, a 23-year-old from Warsaw, who had hidden in a lifeboat when the ship sailed from Kobe, and later mingled with the other passengers.[11]

Rozenberg, who is depicted on the cover of this book, was permitted to land and remain in Australia, and was naturalised five years later.

Australia therefore had a history of dealing with refugees who arrived uninvited, but it had, until the mid 1950s, no experience with those who formally sought asylum in Australia. The Petrovs' was an unusual case in that it did not involve people who had fled their country, but people who, after having lived in Australia for some time, did not want to return home. Because of its geographical position, Australia was initially not affected by the movement of hundreds of people every day who left Eastern Europe to seek refuge in the West. Until 1954, Australia had also had no direct experience with Eastern European defectors.

Les Liveris was the immigration department's representative in Darwin. Although he had not been personally involved, he would have remembered the drama in the early morning of 20 April 1954 at Darwin Airport when police disarmed Evdokia Petrova's Russian escorts. On 26 October 1956, three days after the beginning of the popular uprising in Budapest, Liveris asked his head office for guidance in the event of a repeat of the 1954 incident:

> In view of the present unrest in Europe, it is possible that nationals of Iron Curtain countries may take the opportunity of seeking political asylum during their visit to Australia for the Olympic Games. It is presumed that this matter may already have received consideration, and I would appreciate your early direction as to the action to be taken in the event of any such persons desiring to disembark at Darwin from an outgoing aircraft.[12]

In Canberra, the matter had already received detailed consideration. Senior officers from the prime minister's, immigration, external affairs, treasury and defence departments, and from ASIO, had held several meetings to develop a procedure for handling asylum requests in time for the Melbourne Olympic Games. A few days before Liveris asked for his superiors' direction, Cabinet had:

> approved of the principle that political asylum and refuge should be available in appropriate instances to various categories of aliens namely

> Olympic Games visitors, members of visiting trade and other delegations, members of diplomatic and consular missions in Australia, certain other defectors and Asian leaders.[13]

Cabinet agreed that applications for political asylum be assessed by a committee of review comprising representatives of the Departments of External Affairs and Immigration, and ASIO. But in its 1956 decision, Cabinet also emphasised:

> the need for flexibility in the handling of these matters and the need to keep in touch with ministers and observed that as a general rule any public references to specific cases which might arise should treat them as unexciting incidents which were bound to occur.[14]

Liveris was unaware that the government had considered the issue of asylum and come to a decision, because that decision had not been publicised. The matter had not been debated, either in the media or in parliament. The government's view was that it did not need to be debated. It required an executive decision, to be implemented administratively. No new legislation was needed to create a framework within which the committee assessing asylum applications would operate.

The government also assumed that international law did not require Australia to process requests for asylum in any particular way. The Cabinet submission by the Minister for External Affairs noted:

> Every State has complete jurisdiction over its own territory and the individuals within it. It follows from this principle that every State has absolute discretion concerning the admission of aliens to its territory and thus may not only exclude or expel aliens but admit them, with or without conditions, at will. Competence to grant asylum to defectors or refugees therefore derives directly from the territorial sovereignty of States.[15]

This meant that Australia, as a sovereign state, had the *right* to harbour refugees, and was not obliged to refuse a refugee admission, or extradite him or her, upon the urging of another state. As the submission further noted, this insistence on a state's sovereignty also meant that "no individual has a right to asylum, and the preparedness of a State to grant it in a particular case depends on its relevant domestic law."[16]

The categories of potential asylum seekers mentioned in the Cabinet decision are noteworthy. In a letter to the prime minister (which became an appendix to the Cabinet decision), ASIO's director-general, Charles Spry, distinguished between two types of asylum seekers: defectors and refugees. The former would be "in possession of intelligence that would be of value to Australia or the Western World and that can be exploited." Refugees, on the other hand, would have no intelligence value: their "applications for asylum would be considered on purely humanitarian grounds."[17] On this latter point, Spry disagreed with the Cabinet submission prepared by External Affairs, according to which asylum requests by "refugees" could also be considered favourably because of their propaganda value. But irrespective of this difference, both ASIO and External Affairs differentiated between defectors and refugees according to the precedent set in 1954, when Petrov was identified as a defector, and his wife as a refugee.

When the Australian government agreed on the rules governing its approach to asylum seekers, it could not have known that the developments in Hungary would soon prove its action fortuitous. One of the most memorable events of the Melbourne Olympics was the water polo match between Hungary and the Soviet Union, which had to be called off halfway through because the political tensions between the two countries had erupted into physical violence in the pool. Many Hungarian athletes were dismayed by the events unfolding at home and, while in Melbourne, decided not to return to Hungary.

The government did not expect any propaganda value from requests for political asylum during the Olympic Games. Potential asylum seekers were asked not to lodge their requests until after the closing ceremony on 8 December 1956. By 12 December, 59 members of Olympic delegations, most of them Hungarians, had made it known they would not return home. More than half of them left Australia for the United States to apply for political asylum there. Only nineteen were processed in Australia. All of them were "refugees" rather than "defectors" in Spry's terms. It now became clear that the government's asylum policies were designed for asylum seekers who had either intelligence or propaganda value. The committee established in accordance with the Cabinet decision still classified the nineteen athletes as "political refugees", but they were granted residence permits – much like any other immigrants – rather than political asylum.

The case of the most famous of these asylum seekers illustrates the authorities' approach to "refugees" seeking asylum. Nina Paranyuk was a Ukrainian stewardess on the liner *Gruzia*, which had brought the Soviet Union's Olympic team to Melbourne. On 18 November 1956, while on an organised visit to the Melbourne Zoo, she disappeared. As groups of New Australians had frequently visited the *Gruzia* and challenged its crew to defect, it was assumed she had made an attempt to leave the ship for good and had been assisted to do so. Paranyuk reappeared two months later, long after the *Gruzia* had returned home. She did not apply for political asylum, but the committee of review dealt with her case regardless, and recommended that she be classified as a refugee. But this classification was immaterial, as it was the health, security and character checks that determined a positive outcome for her application for a residence permit.[18]

Between 1956 and 1969, other Eastern Europeans applied for political asylum (or were, like Paranyuk, considered asylum seekers). Most of them were seamen who had deserted their ships. They also included Polish, Czech and Burmese diplomats. None was a defector according to Spry's definition.

During the 1950s and 1960s, Australia was also approached on several occasions to provide asylum to prominent political figures. In 1955, a law firm in Managua, Nicaragua, contacted the Department of Immigration to seek approval for the immigration of one of its clients. According to the lawyers, their client had "had a successful military career," had "a knowledge of three languages," would be "an asset to his country of adoption," and was "a gentleman of independent means."[19] The department decided that they could not admit the gentleman in question, the former president of Argentina, Juan Domingo Perón, who had just been deposed in a military coup. While Perón did not apply for political asylum, and the department did not make a decision about whether or not to grant him asylum, it would have been clear to the government that approving the request would have amounted to granting asylum. In fact, the Department of Immigration's secretary, Tasman Heyes, later defended himself against the charge of not having consulted the Department of External Affairs in the matter by arguing that he had wanted to act quickly "to forestall any local charge that [the government] was negotiating or seriously considering the request."[20]

Three years later, the United States government asked whether Australia would be willing to accommodate another deposed Latin American dictator, Fulgencio Batista of Cuba. The Australian ambassador in Washington learnt that "in the past the United States would have granted political asylum to such ex dictators as Batista" but that that policy had "produced increasing embarrassment" for its government. The United States government hoped that, given "the absence of any important political and other ties," Australia would be spared such embarrassment if it assisted with the "difficult dilemma."[21] Once again, the answer was negative. "Australia," the Australian ambassador told a representative of the United States, "is not in the situation of a country of traditional asylum and an unprecedented decision of this nature would attract much interest and public comment." The Australian authorities were also mindful of the possibility that the admission of an ex-dictator "with a record of violation of human rights" would be contrasted unfavourably with the White Australia policy.[22] As in the case of Perón, the merits of Batista's status as an exile, if not a refugee, did not enter the equation.

The Americans again sought help in 1965, asking Australia to accept two of their staunchest allies in Indochina, Laotian army commander Phoumi Nosavan and Laotian police chief Siho Lamfuthacul, who had staged an unsuccessful coup against the government in Vientiane and then fled to Thailand. The Menzies government did not agree to that request either, even though the 1956 Cabinet decision on political asylum, which was still valid, allowed for the admission of Asian leaders.[23]

Throughout its history, Australia has avoided burdening itself with prominent exiles. To my knowledge, the only two high-profile political figures granted permission to settle in Australia were the former Russian prime minister, Alexander Kerensky, who lived in Australia for about a year in 1945 and 1946, and, more recently, the

East Timorese independence leader, José Ramos-Horta. Kerensky was not offered political asylum. In fact, his first application to visit Australia was refused. In 1945, Australia granted him a six-month visa only in order to allow him and his Australian-born wife, Nell Tritton, to visit her parents in Brisbane.[24]

•

The successful asylum seekers mentioned so far were all nationals of countries under communist rule. There were others. Over several months in late 1961 and early 1962, the case of three Portuguese sailors who sought asylum in Darwin prompted headlines and inspired public comment across Australia. Next to the cases of the Petrovs in 1954 and the Bakhtiyari family in more recent years, it was the most publicised asylum case in Australian history. On 10 December 1961, Joaquim Teixeira, Jose Manuel da Costa and Norberto Augusto Andrade deserted the Portuguese frigate *Goncalves Zarco* and went into hiding in Darwin. In line with government policy on deserters, the Department of External Affairs informed the Portuguese Chargé d'Affaires, Manuel d'Almeida Coutinho – as the local representative of the ship's owner – of the desertion and requested that he arrange for the sailors' repatriation once they were apprehended. Coutinho in turn asked the Australian authorities to take the necessary steps for their apprehension and deportation. On 14 December, three days after the frigate had left Darwin, Teixeira, da Costa and Andrade asked the Northern Territory Administrator for political asylum.[25]

While it was ASIO's responsibility to assess any asylum claims, the decision about whether or not to grant political asylum to the sailors rested with the Department of External Affairs and its minister. After receiving advice from ASIO that the men "could not be regarded in any sense as 'defectors'," the department's secretary, Arthur Tange, reported on 19 December that there were no grounds to grant asylum to the sailors and recommended that they be deported.[26] On 21 December, just before handing responsibility for external affairs to Garfield Barwick, Menzies endorsed Tange's recommendation and agreed that the sailors be deported.[27] The implementation of that decision – that is, the actual deportations – was the responsibility of the

Minister for Immigration, Alexander Downer. He disagreed with Menzies's decision, but signed the deportation orders.

On 4 January 1962, External Affairs informed Coutinho that asylum had not been granted and that the men would be deported to Dili on the next available flight. They were apprehended and transferred to Darwin's Fannie Bay Jail. On 9 January, a Darwin lawyer instituted habeas corpus proceedings in the Northern Territory Supreme Court, challenging the deportation orders. The immigration, attorney-general's and external affairs departments agreed that the deportation be deferred to allow the legal action to proceed.

The Portuguese asylum seekers attracted much public sympathy. There were rallies in Sydney and Brisbane, trade unions inundated the government with telegrams, newspaper editorials all over the country demanded the sailors' release, and many individual Australians wrote letters of protest to the government. Few public voices in Australia doubted that a ruthless dictator ruled Portugal, and that the three sailors had reason to be fearful about returning and should be allowed to stay in Australia. Even an internal briefing paper written in February 1962 by an officer from the Department of External Affairs' European section was blunt in its assessment: "Portugal economically and politically is probably the most backward country in non-Communist Europe... The present regime... is essentially a dictatorship."[28]

Barwick was not prepared to alter Menzies' decision: "I thought that we owed it to a friendly power – Portugal is the oldest (and continuing) ally of Great Britain – to return to its custody deserting members of its defence force."[29] But in his capacity as attorney-general, he came to realise that it would be "wrong in law" to use the deportation provisions of the Immigration Act and hand over the sailors to the Portuguese authorities.[30]

In March, Barwick persuaded the Portuguese government to dismiss the three sailors from the navy and to drop its request for their deportation to Portugal or one of its colonies. His argument was that Portugal's insistence on their return would cause the Australian media to dwell on the nature of the Portuguese regime.[31] As Barwick later wrote in his memoirs, he was "not prepared to accept the journalists' assertions as to the characteristics of [Salazar's] rule."[32] Welcoming the

Portuguese government's decision to dismiss the sailors and seemingly anxious to assure it of his sympathies, he told Coutinho "that the communists, who might have otherwise continued their efforts to cause embarrassment over the ratings" had now turned their attention to other causes.[33] Barwick was still intent on abiding by Menzies's decision, but sought to deport the men instead to Brazil, which had previously welcomed a prominent critic of the Salazar regime.

The attempt to have the deportation orders nullified by the Supreme Court failed, and on 30 April 1962, the High Court rejected the Portuguese sailors' application for leave to appeal the Supreme Court's decision. In his diary, the head of the immigration department, Peter Heydon, recorded that after the High Court decision, "Barwick and Downer had decided to explore Brazil as a possible place of asylum and to make an announcement to this effect without mentioning Brazil."[34] Heydon had opposed the deportation of the Portuguese all along. He wrote two strongly worded memorandums to Downer, warning him that an approach to Brazil would "put us in a ridiculous light in many countries."[35] Only an announcement that the sailors were allowed to stay would protect "the Government from all sorts of emotional and illogical Press exhortation and criticism."[36] Downer himself felt strongly about the Portuguese; subsequently, a *Sunday Mirror* journalist went so far as to claim that he had been prepared to resign over the issue.[37] In a late-night horse-trading session, Barwick finally agreed to let the sailors stay in Australia without granting them political asylum. He accepted the humanitarian argument, even if he did not share it.

Consideration of Australia's international reputation had little influence on the decision to let the sailors stay. In the end, Barwick's concerns about the relationship with Portugal did not have much impact either. The decisive factor was the public campaign in support of the three men's claim for asylum. The government did not want to be seen to disregard the humanitarian argument. Many Australians sympathised with the Portuguese sailors and thought that Australia had a moral obligation to assist them. That the three men were white, young and healthy would have counted in their favour, but their suitability as immigrants was never cited as the main argument in favour of letting them stay.

•

The government's reply to Jim Mulvihill's question was incorrect. Dozens of people "did a Petrov" after Petrov. Why then did the Department of Immigration get its facts wrong? I suspect that the officers researching the issue still considered asylum in terms of Spry's 1954 distinction between refugees and defectors. Only the latter were true asylum seekers. And in that sense, the reply was accurate; Petrov had been the only defector in Spry's sense.

CHAPTER 5

Border crossers

Australian colonial rule in the Pacific has attracted comparatively little attention from historians. Although Papua New Guinea is Australia's closest neighbour, there is scant historical understanding informing the public debate about the relationship between the two countries. When in late 2001, for example, the Australian government cajoled Papua New Guinea into accommodating asylum seekers on Manus Island as part of its "Pacific solution", neither the government nor the media referred to the fact that a camp on Manus had once before, in the late 1960s and early 1970s, housed asylum seekers who had unlawfully entered Australian territory. And when commentators have identified precedents for Australia's treatment of asylum seekers in the past five years, they have pointed to the Indochinese "boat people" who arrived in Australia from 1976 onwards, rather than to the thousands of West Papuan refugees who crossed into the Australian Territory of Papua and New Guinea between 1962 and 1973.

In 1962, the Dutch bowed to international pressure and withdrew from West New Guinea, the last remnant of their former colonial empire in Southeast Asia. For a few months, a United Nations interim administration controlled the western half of the island of New Guinea. On 1 May 1963, control of what became known as West Irian passed to Indonesia. The Sukarno government agreed to hold a referendum, in which the people of West Irian would be allowed to decide about their future. This referendum, the Act of Free Choice, took place in 1969, but it did not allow West Papuans to choose freely between independence and incorporation into Indonesia; its outcome, however, legitimised the latter. In 1969, western New Guinea became the Indonesian province of Irian Jaya.

During the last years of Dutch colonial rule, an indigenous elite had been encouraged to prepare for autonomy and eventual independence. When Indonesia took control of West New Guinea, many of those supposedly liberated from Dutch tutelage resented the fact that one colonial regime was merely supplanted by another. To make matters worse, the new colonial power was not inclined to allow for the possibility of West New Guinea's independence, and was not able to invest nearly as much in the country's economic development as the Dutch had done.

West Papuan aspirations for independence contrasted sharply with Indonesia's plans for the western half of New Guinea. Indonesia, under both Sukarno and Suharto, did not tolerate agitation for West Papuan independence or West Papuan criticism of its administration. The Indonesian security forces imprisoned, and sometimes murdered, perceived opponents of Indonesian rule. Indonesia also adopted a heavy-handed approach in its dealings with ordinary villagers. It was therefore not surprising that from 1962 onwards, an ever-growing number of people fled western New Guinea.

The Australian government had anticipated that, following a Dutch withdrawal, there would be an exodus of refugees from West New Guinea, including Dutch citizens, and also Indonesians and West Papuans who had collaborated with the Dutch. Most of them were thought to be entering the Australian Territory en route to Holland; but, as an External Affairs submission to Cabinet explained in July 1962, it seemed likely that:

> a number of West New Guinea Natives (Papuans) among these "political" refugees would prefer to remain in Papua-New Guinea rather than be removed to Holland or other Dutch territory and it is not improbable that the Dutch... would look on this as a desirable "solution"... As regards the Papuans (natives of West New Guinea) it is felt that in view of the comparatively small number thought to be likely to be involved (apparently about 150) requests for permission to remain in Australian Papua-New Guinea could be considered and each case

> decided upon its merits by the Minister for Territories in consultation with the Minister for External Affairs... Specific individual requests for political asylum could be considered each on its merits. Although these persons would clearly be a responsibility of the Dutch, there are nevertheless humanitarian reasons with which the Australian public would probably sympathise for not insisting on the expatriation overseas of natives of the island of New Guinea.[1]

External Affairs wrote the submission before the Dutch and Indonesian agreement about an orderly handover and thus at a time when an emergency evacuation of the Dutch and their allies seemed likely. The submission noted that these suggestions only applied if there were as few West Papuan refugees as estimated, and that there could well be more. On 6 August 1962 – after Jakarta and The Hague had reached an agreement – Cabinet approved the proposals set out in the submission.

In the first two years after the Dutch left West New Guinea, Australia only accepted West Papuan refugees who were sponsored by the Dutch. These were usually people who had worked for the colonial authorities and were known for their anti-Indonesian sentiments. Some of them went into exile in Holland, others were allowed to remain in the Australian Territory but were financially supported by the Dutch government. This latter group became known as the "Dutch pensioners." With the exception of an ethnic Chinese family who fled West New Guinea in April 1963, all others who crossed the border into Papua and New Guinea in 1963 and the first half of 1964 were sent back by Australian officials. In the first year after the Indonesians took control of West New Guinea from the United Nations, from June 1963 to May 1964, 377 "non-political native refugees" crossed the border without a valid visa. According to the Department of Territories, they left West New Guinea mainly for one of two reasons: "general dislike of [the] Indonesian administration," or "avoidance of conscription."[2]

In March 1964, the Department of Territories drafted a policy statement, which was approved by its minister, Charles Edward ("Ceb") Barnes. It drew a clear distinction between "political" and "non-political" refugees: the former being "persons who engaged in political activities before the Dutch withdrawal of a kind which the

Dutch considered would place these people in jeopardy," the latter being West Papuans who crossed the border merely to live under Australian rather than Indonesian rule. "Non-political refugees" – who, according to the minister's understanding, included persons engaged in political activities *after* the Indonesian takeover – were to be returned to West Irian because:

> The fact is that, by an international decision to which Australia was party, West New Guinea is under Indonesian Administration and the people of West New Guinea and the Administration of Papua and New Guinea alike have to learn to live with that situation. To allow permanent movement across the border for dissidents to settle in the Australian Territory could start migration of such numbers as might burden the people receiving them and create administrative and other problems in our own Territory, and at the same time give grounds for suspicion on the part of the Indonesian Administration that this was deliberate and ill-meant, thereby impairing neighbourly relations.[3]

The implementation of the government's policy was fraught with difficulties. The terrain, and the constraints imposed by Australia's very limited presence in the border region, made it impossible for patrol officers to police the border effectively. Refugees sent back sometimes returned to Australian territory and remained there in hiding for as long as the local villagers tolerated them. And the "border crossers," as the refugees were often referred to, probably knew that the Australian Territory's police escorting them to the border would not shoot at them if they slipped back into Papua and New Guinea. Patrol officers sometimes took pity on them. In September 1964, assistant district officer A. M. Bottrill judged three refugees to be "in such a dejected and desperate mood" that he sent them to a border village rather than back to West Irian.[4] But they, too, were eventually returned, after the district commissioner found that "[Bottrill's] heart got the better of him."[5]

Among those returned to Indonesia was a group of fifteen West Papuans who had fled to Papua and New Guinea in early 1964. Their leader was a teacher, Fred Mandowen. In a statement, he outlined the reasons for requesting asylum in the Australian Territory:

> Those who do not like Indonesia and who say that they are Papuans and won't acknowledge that they are Indonesians are gaoled and shot. If someone keeps the Papuan flag he is gaoled. We do not want Indonesia. We want to remain Papuans... Because the Indonesians are looking for us, we fled here so that we escape the punishment and ill-treatment of Indonesia. We wish to come and stay here and work here till the Indonesian government has left West Papua then we can return. Because if we stay in West Papua with Indonesia it is possible that we will be gaoled or killed.[6]

Mandowen and his group were in touch with Lutheran missionary teachers who had previously worked in West New Guinea and had since returned to the Australian Territory. When the missionaries learnt that the West Papuans were to be repatriated, they appealed to the Australian government. They were able to confirm that dissidents suffered persecution at the hands of the Indonesians. The Departments of Territories and External Affairs took the appeal seriously, if only because of concerns that "the letter [could] reach the press" and be the trigger for West Irian becoming "a major public issue in Australia."[7] The reason Barnes cited for rejecting the missionaries' appeal is revealing. He informed the missionaries that:

> The statements which these students made to Administration officers did not demonstrate that they themselves had suffered or had been in actual danger on account of any political activities which we would normally regard as legitimate. There was in short nothing to justify by international standards granting them refuge in Papua and New Guinea.[8]

Because the Australian government considered Indonesia's occupation of the western half of New Guinea to be legitimate, it deemed anti-Indonesian protests against the status quo to be illegitimate. Persecution on account of illegitimate activities, Barnes suggested, disqualified refugees for political asylum.

In December 1964, Djoni Jakedewa became the first West Papuan refugee not sponsored by the Dutch who fled after Indonesia assumed control of West Irian and was allowed to remain in Papua and New

Guinea. Together with his employers, the Moluccan Nikijuluw family, he had landed at Wutung in New Guinea's Sepik District in September 1964. The Indonesians had killed Jakedewa's father, mother and uncles, possibly because of the father's association with West Papuan nationalists. The Australian district commissioner in Wewak thought it was also possible that these murders had been the result of previous failed attempts by Jakedewa to cross into Papua and New Guinea.[9] Partly because of the murders, and partly because of fears of adverse publicity, the Department of Territories successfully recommended that Jakedewa be granted a five-year residence permit for the Australian Territory.[10]

Several of Benjamin Nikijuluw's family were associated with the South Moluccan rebels and were living in exile in Holland. He and his wife and children were initially allowed to remain in Papua and New Guinea because the Australian government hoped the Dutch would accept them, too. His claims that he had been persecuted were not as strong as those of some of the West Papuans who had been returned to West Irian in 1963 and 1964. But ASIO's director-general, Charles Spry, felt that Nikijuluw was a genuine refugee because he had left considerable assets behind without any hope of recovering them once he entered the Australian Territory.[11] In February 1966, after the Dutch government had declined Nikijuluw's application for permission to settle in Holland, he and his family were granted permissive residence in Papua and New Guinea – despite Indonesian protests, claims that Nikijuluw had embezzled public funds and slept with his uncle's stepdaughter, and demands that he be deported to Indonesia to face criminal charges.[12]

After December 1964, other refugees were allowed to remain in Papua and New Guinea if they could convince the Australian authorities that they had been politically active in West Irian and had been persecuted by the Indonesians. According to Australian government statistics, 573 people crossed the border illegally between 1963 and 1966. The Department of Territories recorded 866 illegal border crossings in 1967, and 801 in 1968.[13] These statistics should be regarded with some caution. When asked in 1971 about the number of West Papuans Australia had returned to Irian Jaya, Ceb Barnes said: "Because of the nature of the border between Indonesia and Papua

New Guinea it is not possible to state the number of people who move across it in either direction."[14]

While not formally granting any request for political asylum, between 1962 and August 1969 Australia allowed 75 West Irianese and their families to stay in Papua and New Guinea on five-year permissive residence visas. By June 1970, that number had increased to 135. Their number included the "Dutch pensioners." By the time the Australian Territory was granted self-government in 1973, some 500 West Papuan permissive residents were living in Papua and New Guinea.

After their acceptance of Jakedewa had set a precedent, the Australian authorities distinguished between three different types of border crossers: (a) "Ordinary inland village people, still fairly primitive, who cross the border for purposes such as hunting, subsistence agriculture or visiting people of their clan"; (b) "Unskilled, semi-sophisticates generally with limited primary school education who are half-heartedly looking for employment and a higher standard of living" (that is, in today's parlance, "economic refugees"); and (c) "Genuine refugees."[15] The latter were able to convince the Australian authorities that they were being persecuted for their political beliefs, and that they were sufficiently educated not to belong in either of the first two categories. The granting of permissive residence seemed also to depend on the refugees' education, willingness to work and employment prospects – even though their stay was meant to be temporary, and they were never supposed to enter Australia proper.

Lazarus Itaar was one such refugee granted permissive residency. On several occasions, the Indonesians had imprisoned Itaar because of his membership of the OPM – the Organisasi Papua Merdeka (Free Papua Movement), an independence movement fighting the Indonesians since 1964 – and his contact with other dissidents. He feared for his life. On 9 February 1968 and then again on 15 March, he unlawfully entered Papua and New Guinea. On both occasions, the Australians returned him to the border. Itaar tried a third time on 8 April. This time, his request for political asylum was processed, and he was allowed to remain in the Australian Territory while his case was being investigated. Such an investigation typically involved an interview by a Special Branch officer, who then made a recommendation to the Department of Territories about whether or not a border crosser should be allowed to remain in Papua and New Guinea. In Itaar's case, the interviewing officer found:

> On the last time he was returned to the border he showed all the signs of being filled with terror at the prospect of having to re-enter Indonesian controlled territory. He is a clean sober person and is a practising Christian... He has been medically examined and has been found to have a normal state of health.[16]

As his fear did not stop the authorities from repatriating him on a previous occasion, it is possible, or even likely, that his education, skills, employability, state of health and Christian beliefs played no small part in the officer's recommendation to let Itaar remain in the Territory.

Four main factors informed the harsh line taken in 1963 and 1964, and the very selective acceptance of refugees from 1965. First, the Australian government was afraid of a mass influx of refugees from Indonesia, and was anxious not to encourage the movement of people across the border. Second, it did not want to burden a future independent Papua New Guinea either with a large number of potentially undesirable residents, or with a strained relationship with Indonesia.

Third, and perhaps most importantly, Australia was determined to retain or establish a harmonious relationship with its powerful north-western neighbour. The Cabinet submission of 1962, from which I have quoted above, already noted the potential implications of Australia's acceptance of refugees for its relationship with Indonesia:

> It is recognised that as [West Papuan refugees] would be leaving West New Guinea for political reasons, the reception of these persons or some of them could possibly give rise to difficulties e.g. if the Indonesian Government were to demand their surrender, or if their presence stimulated anti-Indonesian agitation among inhabitants of Papua-New Guinea.

The submission suggested a way to defuse a potentially embarrassing situation: "It could however be made a condition that persons so received should not engage in any political activity."[17] The government adopted this proposal: Australia granted permissive residence visas to the Dutch-sponsored refugees and those whose asylum claims it accepted only if they signed an undertaking not to engage in anti-Indonesian political activity during their stay in Papua and New Guinea.

Permissive residence visas did not entitle their holders to travel to Australia. Permissive residents were also barred from settling in the border region and, sometimes, told where to live. In 1968, the Territory's administration directed more than 50 West Papuan permissive residents to move to a camp at Lorengau on Manus Island. A journalist visiting them in 1969 reported:

> [T]he status of temporary still remains with all the uncertainties, frustrations, confusions and despair... For six months, they have sat on this island coast, limited by language and isolated by distance and their own inability to help themselves... The men were sullen and silent, with six months of decaying idleness behind them and an indefinite period of the same ahead.[18]

The fourth factor in the government's approach to West Papuan refugees – which served in some way to ease the effects of the first three – was that the government was wary of adverse public opinion in Australia and the Territory. For example, while his department was contemplating whether or not to grant political asylum to Nikijuluw, a senior External Affairs officer pointed out that "if we do not give him asylum, the matter will arouse considerable press and public attention with attendant complications for relations with Indonesia."[19] Similarly, the Minister for Territories accepted the advice of the Administrator of Papua and New Guinea that Nikijuluw's forcible return could result in the refugee's suicide and could therefore generate "wide publicity which would open the way to all sorts of misrepresentation and criticism."[20]

In Papua and New Guinea, the plight of West Papuan asylum seekers met with a sympathetic response from many expatriates, from members of the indigenous elite, and from people living in the border region, particularly those in the Sepik District.[21] In Australia, typical critics of the government's position were not left-wing trade unionists, as had been the case with the three Portuguese sailors in 1961–62, but rather some of the government's own supporters. In 1965, the Mount Gambier Voters' Policy Association, a group of self-professed "Liberal Party R.S.L. men," expressed concern over press reports that West Papuan refugees had been returned to West Irian. "Do you not think it appalling that we return these refugees for execution?" the association asked the Minister for External Affairs (and former Minister for Territories), Paul Hasluck:

> To say they are illegal immigrants is deplorable, and to force their return for health reasons is no excuse for us being a party to their murdur [*sic*]! These unfortunates could be quarantined or innoculated [*sic*] the same as any other human.[22]

It was not accidental that the Liberal voters from Mount Gambier were also returned soldiers. In another letter to the Minister for External Affairs in 1965, a correspondent demanded that West Papuan refugees be allowed to stay in the Australian Territory, for: "Many of our soldiers during the war owed their lives to the care, and help, and carrying on stretchers over rough mountain ranges by these natives."[23]

But these letters of protest need to be put in perspective. During the 1960s, there were no public demonstrations of solidarity with West Papuan refugees, and their plight attracted not nearly as much attention in Australia as that of the Afghan and Iraqi refugees in 2001, or that of the Hungarian refugees in 1956 and 1957. Even in comparison with the outcry provoked by the decision to deport the three Portuguese sailors who sought political asylum in 1961, public declarations of support for the West Papuans were rather muted. The government's sensitivity to domestic criticism of its response to West Papuan refugees is therefore the more remarkable.

The desire not to offend the Indonesians, and the desire not to offend the public in Australia and Papua and New Guinea, were related. In January 1963, the Minister for External Affairs, Garfield Barwick, summoned the Indonesian ambassador to let him know that he, the minister:

> was greatly concerned by the Papuans who were presenting themselves at the border in considerable numbers – some complaining of

> ill-treatment by Indonesian officials – others merely apprehensive because of what they had heard of Indonesian conduct. His present thinking was that these Papuans should be returned to West New Guinea, but the situation was difficult. It was to the interest of both sides to avoid a mass movement of population. But if the numbers and circumstances of the people seeking political asylum evoked humanitarian considerations public opinion in Australia would react sharply and the Australian government could not take a rigid or seemingly harsh line. It was therefore important that the apprehensions of the West Papuans should not be aroused.[24]

The Australian government was worried about its own image, and about that of the Indonesians. The Department of External Affairs sometimes supported requests for admission to Papua and New Guinea with the argument that a refusal could provoke criticism in the media and draw attention to the very conditions in West Irian that had prompted the flight across the border. The government was afraid it could be compelled to take a tougher stand against Indonesia to placate public opinion in Australia.

The available evidence suggests that Australian ministers and senior bureaucrats did not make their decisions about West Papuan refugees on humanitarian grounds, or in response to Indonesia's appalling human rights record. Publicly, however, the government maintained that such considerations did guide its response to the influx of refugees. In August 1962, Barwick answered a question put to him in parliament by the Liberal MP, Wilfrid Kent Hughes: "If any requests are received under the heading of political asylum, they will be entertained and decided on their particular merits from a very high humanitarian point of view in accordance with traditional British principles."[25] But off the public record, the minister distanced himself from these principles. In a directive to his department, Barwick suggested that "[we] should not be too infected with the British notion of being a home for the oppressed."[26]

The Minister for Territories, Ceb Barnes, and his predecessor, Paul Hasluck, also had a narrow understanding of the humanitarian considerations involved. In January 1963, Barwick and Hasluck had agreed that the Administrator in Port Moresby be instructed "to pay careful regard to considerations of humanity and do what he can to avoid any unnecessary distress by the refugees."[27] But, as the Department of Territories' policy statement of March 1964 (from which I have quoted earlier) clarified:

> The consideration of humanity does not come into the decision whether they should be allowed to stay or return if they are not political refugees; it only comes into the execution of the decision that they should return.[28]

In public statements, the government claimed that West Papuan border crossers who were sent back to West Irian came to no harm. On 18 May 1965, the Minister for Territories responded in parliament to the suggestion that returned refugees were being ill-treated in West Irian: "I say very definitely that there is no evidence of this whatsoever."[29] But the files of the Departments of Territories and External Affairs contain references to refugees who had reportedly been beaten, imprisoned or murdered after their return to West Irian. One day after the minister's emphatic response, Djoni Jakedewa's brother Mesak was sent back across the border. The Territory's Local Intelligence Committee believed that he was killed by Indonesian troops within less than a month of his return.[30]

On 16 February 1969, eight West Papuan refugees arrived by raft on Moa (Banks Island) in the Torres Strait. Their journey from a camp near the border between Papua and West Irian had taken them 34 days. One man had died during that trip. This was the first (but by no means last) case of West Papuans applying for asylum in Australia itself. Their arrival presented the authorities with a dilemma. Neither the Department of Immigration nor External Affairs wanted to create a precedent by processing West Papuan applications for asylum in Australia. Instead, both wanted to remove the men "quickly and quietly" to Papua and New Guinea, where their requests could be dealt with.[31] But the authorities were aware that the enforced removal of the men, whose arrival had already been noted by the Australian media, could generate negative publicity. They therefore depended on the asylum seekers' cooperation.

The case was complicated further by the fact that five of the men had earlier entered the Territory and been granted permissive residence visas, and then in 1968 returned to West Irian. One of them explained that his return was the "result of a Radio Australia newscast to the effect that the United Nations would move into West Irian to supervise the act of free choice in 1969" and that he believed that West Irian would again be administered by the United Nations.[32]

On 21 February, a Brisbane-based officer of the Department of Immigration was charged with the delicate task of persuading the eight refugees to agree to their removal to the Territory. Two days later, this immigration official met the men on Thursday Island. He told them that the Australian government had decided they would not be allowed to remain in Australia, including the Torres Strait Islands. He later described how he put the situation to them:

> I then... made the offer to send them to Papua New Guinea where they could fully state their case. They appeared lukewarm to my offer and asked if they could discuss the matter between themselves. After about fifteen minutes Mr. Toembay asked if they could be sent to the Netherlands. I told him that his request could be raised if and when they went to Papua New Guinea & if they did not accept my offer to go to Papua New Guinea, the Immigration Department would have no alternative but to give serious consideration to their being returned to West Irian.[33]

Reluctantly the men agreed to be flown the following day to Papua and New Guinea. When the Labor MP, Jim Cairns, raised the issue in parliament two weeks later, the Minister for External Affairs, Gordon Freeth, could report that the men had voluntarily gone to Papua and New Guinea.[34]

There, they were processed much like other border crossers. Alexander Toembay, who acted as spokesperson for the group, was one of those who had lived in the Territory before. In his report about Toembay's application for permissive residence, the interviewing officer wrote:

> [H]e is genuinely terrified of returning to MERAUKE where he reckons the INDONESIANS would definitely harm him. I do not doubt this as he was well known to the Indonesians even before his attempt to get into Australia permanently in the raft episode.[35]

But the Administrator in Port Moresby recommended that all eight applications for political asylum be refused. He argued that the political situation in West Irian had not deteriorated since Toembay and others had returned in 1968, and that they had only themselves to blame if they were persecuted by the Indonesians: "In fact, it is only because of their continued anti-Indonesian attitudes, unwillingness to adapt to the regime there, that their future may be compromised." The Administrator also regarded the five who had previously spent time in the Territory as undesirable migrants: "they are lazy, unwilling to work or assimilate, have an exaggerated opinion of their own importance and capabilities, and hold the Australian Government responsible for much of what has happened to them."[36] The Minister for Territories concurred with the Administrator's recommendation.

Overall, comparatively few West Papuans sought asylum in Australia rather than in Papua and New Guinea. But arguably, Australian asylum seeker and refugee policies have for almost half a century been informed by the fear of large numbers of refugees entering Australia as the country of first asylum. Such a fear is more realistic now, with politically volatile conditions both in Papua New Guinea and in Indonesia, than in, say, 1969. But government officials were aware of Australia's potential as a country of first asylum even before the arrival of the West Papuan raft-men on Moa. In 1958, a senior External Affairs officer wondered aloud whether "it is just conceivable that we shall be confronted with isolated requests for political asylum by Indonesians belonging to the dissident movement."[37] At the time, no such request eventuated. But the determination of the Departments of External Affairs and Immigration that the raft-men's applications for political asylum not be processed in Australia suggests they did not want to give potential asylum seekers grounds for assuming that Australia would be willing to play a role as a country of first asylum.

CHAPTER 6

Convention refugees

In recent years, Australia's relationship with the United Nations High Commissioner for Refugees (UNHCR) has been strained. The UNHCR has been highly critical of Australia's mandatory detention regime, particularly as it involves the detention of children. It has also criticised the "Pacific solution," whereby Australia sent people seeking its protection to prison camps in Papua New Guinea and Nauru, both former colonies heavily dependent on Australian foreign aid. It is often assumed that Australia's relationship with the UNHCR has soured only recently. Both the Australian government and its critics regularly point out that historically Australia was one of the UNHCR's staunchest supporters. However, a critical examination of the evidence shows that, before 1973, Australia's support for the UNHCR and the principles promoted by that organisation was, at best, erratic. This is particularly evident on examination of Australia's role in the establishment of the UNHCR and in the drafting of the 1951 Refugee Convention, and of Australia's cooperation with the UNHCR over refugees in Papua and New Guinea.

The UNHCR is the latest in a succession of international agencies charged with alleviating the plight of refugees. In 1920, the League of Nations appointed the Norwegian explorer, Fridtjof Nansen, as the first High Commissioner for Refugees. His task was initially limited to finding a solution to the problem of Russian refugees. Under different names and with varying responsibilities, the High Commissioner's office functioned until 1946, although it had virtually no impact on the refugee crises of the 1930s and 1940s that were triggered by the policies of Nazi Germany. Another international agency, the Intergovernmental Committee on Refugees, was set up in 1938 as a result of the Evian conference (see Chapter 1). It, too, proved ineffective.

In 1943, the Allies established the United Nations Relief and Rehabilitation Administration (UNRRA) because they correctly assumed that they would have to care for large numbers of displaced civilians once they began to dislodge Axis troops from areas they had occupied during the war. Australia was prominently involved in the UNRRA and was the fourth-largest contributor to its funds. Its contribution was significant; as Charles Price has pointed out, it represented "the first really large sum the Australian government had ever given for refugee work abroad."[1] Unlike the League's High Commissioner and the Intergovernmental Committee on Refugees, the UNRRA was well resourced. Repatriation rather than resettlement was its main task. It was only in late 1945 that the Western powers realised that many of those repatriated by the UNRRA did not want to return to their homelands, and that those who were returned to the Soviet Union often faced persecution. The United States, in particular, became increasingly critical of the work performed by the UNRRA.

In 1946 the United States moved to set up the International Refugee Organisation (IRO), which was given the task of resettling displaced persons (DPs) who refused to be repatriated. Australia abstained in the United Nations General Assembly vote that resulted in the organisation's establishment, but became one of its eighteen member states. The IRO took responsibility for DPs as well as for "escapees," that is, Eastern Europeans who fled communist-ruled countries to settle in the West. Between 1947 and 1952, more than one million people were resettled under the auspices of the IRO. The United States and Australia resettled about half of that number, with Canada and Israel accepting another 25 per cent between them.

When in May 1947 the Australian government decided to join the IRO, it approved a joint submission by the Minister for External Affairs and the Treasurer that noted: "Participation would not involve us in commitments to take refugees into the country, our freedom in this regard being unimpaired."[2] But Arthur Calwell, in particular, soon realised that the IRO could play a major role in supplying Australia with suitable immigrants. Within months of joining the IRO, the government came to appreciate that the IRO enabled Australia to recruit settlers among European refugees on its own terms and very cheaply (see Chapter 2).

The IRO was set up to solve what was thought to be a temporary problem and was always intended to have a short lifespan. In December 1949, the United Nations General Assembly decided that, following the termination of the IRO's activities, an Office of the High Commissioner for Refugees be established from 1 January 1951. Australia contributed to the discussions about the wording of the UNHCR's statute and of the Convention Relating to the Status of Refugees, which were to provide the international legal framework for the High Commissioner's work. Australia was, however, not a member of the Ad Hoc Committee formed in 1949 to prepare the draft for a refugee convention. Throughout the debate that led to the establishment of the UNHCR and the drafting of the Convention, the Australian government was sceptical about the role the UNHCR could play and disagreed strongly with some of the sentiments in the Convention.

Before the 1951 Convention Relating to the Status of Refugees, there had been earlier attempts to codify the rights of refugees. A Convention on Refugees drafted in 1933 obliged signatories not to return refugees to their countries of origin. Although the League of Nations Assembly approved the text in 1934, only nine member states acceded to it. Australia was not one of them.

Australia's objections to the draft 1951 Convention centred on four main issues: the definition of the term "refugee"; the commitment not to discriminate against refugees; the commitment not to penalise those unlawfully entering a country of first asylum; and the commitment not to deport refugees. At the time of drafting, the Department of Immigration articulated these objections with particular vehemence.

The definition of the term "refugee" in the 1951 Convention differed from previous definitions in three main respects: first, it centred on the characteristic of persecution; second, it was, unlike those drafted in the 1920s and 1930s, about individuals rather than about groups; and third, it was potentially universal. Australia was primarily concerned about the latter aspect. Commenting on a draft of the

Convention, the immigration department's Tasman Heyes wrote in May 1950:

> There are thousands of non-European refugees, and acceptance by Australia of a convention which provided that such a class of persons should not be discriminated against and should not be subject to any penalty for illegal entry, would be a direct negation of the immigration policy followed by all Australian Governments since Federation.[3]

While those drafting the Convention had mainly the plight of Eastern European refugees in mind, one of the largest refugee crises in the immediate postwar years had in fact taken place outside Europe, when some fourteen million people had become displaced on the Indian subcontinent after the partition of India.

Australia was particularly concerned that it would have to accord protection under the Convention to people who entered the country on tourist or student visas but were technically refugees according to the Convention definition. Australia therefore tried to limit the applicability of the Convention. In 1951, Australian negotiators were instructed:

> [A] provision should be inserted in the convention, either in the definition or elsewhere that people who enter a country in some other capacity e.g., as a tourist or student could not, under the convention, automatically assume refugee status subsequently in order to avail themselves of benefits not otherwise available to them.[4]

The Department of Immigration also rejected the Convention articles designed to protect refugees against discrimination, because those the IRO brought to Australia were obliged to enter into two-year work contracts, and were thus treated differently from other Australian residents.

Australia further objected to the article dealing with the unlawful entry of asylum seekers. Although Australia had not yet experienced the arrival of "boat people," the prospect of asylum seekers approaching by sea seemed to have been on Heyes' mind. He wrote:

> This article... is designed to recognise a right of asylum for persons escaping from persecution; but... it merely permits unlawful entry, so long as the refugee presents himself without delay to the authorities and "shows good cause" for his illegal entry. This is obviously designed to meet conditions in Europe where there are frontiers across which a refugee may escape. It would hardly accord with Australia's immigration policy if the Atlantic and Pacific Oceans were to be ranked as frontiers across which asylum should be sought.[5]

And finally, the Convention allowed the expulsion of refugees only when their presence endangered national security or public order. Australia, however, routinely deported non-citizens for a variety of reasons, including mental illness (see Chapter 7). The Australian delegation therefore argued that the Convention would accord preferential treatment to refugees.

In 1950, the UN General Assembly decided that the draft Refugee Convention be put to a special conference of plenipotentiaries. The Australian government, which had opposed this conference, was faced with the question of whether an Australian delegation should attend to try to influence the Convention's final text, or whether Australia should follow New Zealand's lead and boycott the conference to avoid embarrassment over its objections to the Convention. The Department of Immigration argued that Australia's objections to the Convention were unlikely to be met and were of such a fundamental nature that it made no sense to send a delegation.[6] Even the United Nations section of the Department of External Affairs, which favoured Australia's attending the conference, found:

> Australia as a whole will draw no direct advantage from this convention. It confers no benefits upon Australia, other than to give certain protections to "New Australians."... It is very doubtful, even if [Australia's] principal objections... were removed, that Australia would ever ratify the convention.[7]

A total of 25 countries, including Australia, were represented at the Geneva conference in July 1951. No Asian country except Iraq, and no communist-ruled country except Yugoslavia, took part in the deliberations. Although the delegation was careful not to highlight Australia's objections, it was comparatively isolated on account of its opposition to key elements of the draft Convention. Only the United States shared Australia's reservations. At one stage in the negotiations, after the United States delegate tried to argue that the Convention would interfere with the right of migrant-receiving countries to select their immigrants, the Danish chairman pointed out "that the convention had nothing to do with migration." Thereupon the Australian delegate suggested:

> that this should be explicitly stated by a clause to the effect that "nothing in the convention should be regarded as limiting the power of contracting states to legislate in regard to migration." This was strongly opposed.[8]

Yet the Australian and United States delegations were not the only ones attempting to limit the Convention's scope. France suggested amending Article 1 by inserting a qualifier designed to exclude non-Europeans. This proposal was bitterly opposed by the so-called universalists led by Britain, but in the end all delegations except Yugoslavia's agreed to allow contracting states to make the Convention only applicable to people who had become refugees as a result of "events occurring in Europe."[9]

The Australian and United States governments believed that the Refugee Convention would interfere with their immigration laws and were suspicious of the newly created international agency. The United States did not accede to the Convention until the late 1960s, and only began supporting the UNHCR financially in 1955. Both countries were instrumental in the establishment of the Intergovernmental Committee for European Migration, which was conceived as a successor organisation to the IRO and set up in competition to the UNHCR. During the 1950s and 1960s, Australia tended to admit refugees through the Intergovernmental Committee rather than through the UNHCR.

Heyes had recognised that the 1951 Convention paved the way for a universal definition of the term "refugee" and that the UNHCR was the first international agency potentially responsible for dealing with refugees in all parts of the world. But both the UNHCR's statute and the Refugee Convention reflected their historical origins, and the interests of the United States and its allies. These origins were nowhere more apparent than in the wording of the Convention's Article 1, which defines the term "refugee." In his history of the UNHCR, Gil Loescher observes:

> The adoption of persecution as the main characteristic of a refugee was made to fit a Western interpretation of asylum-seekers. The Western states who were chiefly responsible for the persecution-centred definition perceived refugees to be victims of oppressive, totalitarian, and specifically Communist regimes. The definition had the added advantage that it would serve ideological purposes by stigmatizing the fledgling Communist regimes as persecutors.[10]

Australia acceded to the Refugee Convention in 1954. The Department of Immigration dropped many of its initial objections when Australia was able to opt against making the Convention universally applicable. Australia nevertheless recorded reservations regarding six of the Convention's articles. They included a reservation about the provisions of Article 32, which stipulates, among other things, that "[c]ontracting States shall not expel a refugee lawfully in their territory save on grounds of national security or public order."

By 1962, 32 countries had become party to the Convention, 21 of them without stipulating a geographical limitation. By then the number of European "Convention refugees" was comparatively small, and the High Commissioner was anxious to make the Convention universally applicable. In 1965, an international conference in Bellagio recommended that the Convention be amended by a protocol whose main function would be the deletion of the Convention's time and geographical limitations. This Protocol took effect in 1967.

Australia did not sign the Protocol until 1973. An acknowledgment of the universality of the Convention's Article 1, which defined the term "refugee," would have contradicted Australia's restricted immigration policy. But perhaps more importantly, by 1967 Australia faced a refugee problem in its immediate neighbourhood. By signing the Protocol, Australia would have conceded that many of the West

Papuan border crossers were refugees in the terms of the Refugee Convention, and would therefore have implicitly invited the UNHCR's involvement in solving the West Papuan refugee problem. When Australia eventually signed the Protocol, in December 1973, it did so with the reservation that its provisions did not extend to Papua New Guinea.

After becoming a reluctant party to the Convention, Australia continued to oppose any move that could be seen to widen the High Commissioner's powers, in particular with regard to non-European refugees. In 1957, for example, the United States, Taiwan and Britain lobbied United Nations members to support a resolution authorising the High Commissioner to interest himself in the issue of Chinese refugees in Hong Kong, and encouraging other countries to resettle Chinese refugees. The Australian government opposed the latter part of the resolution because of Australia's non-European immigration policy, and the former "because of doubt as to the High Commissioner's mandate, and difficulty of distinguishing between refugees and impoverished Chinese non refugees."[11] It was only because Australia did not want to be isolated as the only Western country siding with the Soviet bloc that the Australian delegation eventually voted in favour of a watered-down version of the resolution.[12]

Australia's relations with the UNHCR were put to the test when Australia, or rather its territory, Papua and New Guinea, became a country of first asylum after the Dutch withdrawal from West New Guinea in 1962. In May and June 1963 – just after an Indonesian administration had replaced the United Nations interim administration – the High Commissioner, Felix Schnyder, made an official visit to Australia. He met the prime minister, the secretary of the Department of External Affairs, and other high-ranking government officials. There is no indication in the archival record that Schnyder raised the issue of West Papuan refugees with the Australian government. It may be that he was simply unaware of the problem. There is no indication either that the Australians briefed Schnyder about that issue. This is more noteworthy given that the situation in western New Guinea had preoccupied the Australian government in the early 1960s and led to a Cabinet decision determining Australia's response to Dutch, Indonesian and West Papuan refugees (see Chapter 5).

The first piece of evidence suggesting that the UNHCR was becoming concerned about the flight of West Papuans dates from March 1965. By then, Australia had turned away hundreds of border crossers. On 2 March, the UNHCR's representative for Australia and New Zealand, Alexander McIver, wrote to the Department of External Affairs to enquire what the Minister for Territories had meant when – in an interview with the *Sunday Telegraph* – he had emphasised the "need to recognise international Conventions." Did he perhaps refer to the 1951 Refugee Convention?[13] Not having received a reply, McIver followed his first letter up with another two weeks later, in which he quoted the UNHCR's legal adviser, Paul Weis, whose interest had been sparked by a reference to West Papuan refugees in a London newspaper. Weis noted that while the 1951 Convention did not apply to West Papuan refugees, "they could, on the merits, be regarded as refugees within the High Commissioner's mandate" and "the High Commissioner could extend his good offices to them." Weis also pointed out that the "principle of non-refoulement... should apply regardless of the Convention status of the persons concerned."[14]

Australian officials were anxious to reassure the UNHCR. In reply to McIver's first query, assistant secretary Bob Furlonger said that the Minister for Territories had referred to conventions "only in the sense of 'accepted international practices' and had no specific International Convention in mind." He also acquainted McIver with the government's official line on West Papuan border crossers:

> There is at present no refugee problem in New Guinea. Indeed, the word "refugee" is largely inapplicable to the kind of cross border movement that has taken place between West Irian and the Territory of Papua and New Guinea. Those persons who have come across the border have in most cases been resident in the border area, with many of them having tribal connections and tribal lands extending across the border into Papua/New Guinea. Papuans in other categories have in nearly all cases agreed to return to West Irian after discussing their situation with officials of our Administration. Over the last year, only one of these cases involved a request by a Papuan for entry on political grounds.[15]

As demonstrated in the last chapter, this representation of the situation was patently untrue. On the day he replied to McIver, Furlonger also contacted Australia's representative in Geneva, Brian Hill:

> I have no need to labour the question of the delicacy of our relationship with Indonesia in New Guinea and the problems which would be created for us by any ill-considered action, particularly if taken publicly, by the High Commissioner's Office... It is important that UNHCR appreciate the problems arising from our unique position as a country of Western European background living alongside an Asian country – and a particularly turbulent one at that.

Furlonger asked Hill to speak to Schnyder and to Thomas Jamieson, the UNHCR's director of operations, about "the refugee question in New Guinea":

> [W]e expect that no action would be contemplated by the High Commissioner's Office – even in the form of references in UNHCR documents – without the closest consultation with us. I think that Schnyder and Jamieson would appreciate the force of this view; what needs also to be avoided is that people like Weis, who may not realise the political sensitivity of the matter, may take seemingly routine action at a lower level which could be just as embarrassing as action taken with the full knowledge of senior UNHCR people.[16]

Jamieson promised Hill that there would be no references to West Papuan refugees in UNHCR documents and that "officers down the line knew the position."[17] The episode says much about the UNHCR's dependence on countries such as Australia, which made significant financial contributions to the organisation, had traditionally offered a substantial number of resettlement places, and was a long-serving member of the UNHCR's executive and advisory committees. Jamieson, and possibly Schnyder, were easily cajoled into ignoring the refugee issue in Papua and New Guinea. Their local representative, McIver, was sufficiently aware of the sensitivity of the issue to have waited until early 1965 before first officially raising it with the Australian government.

In the long term, however, the High Commissioner could not ignore the refugee issue in Papua and New Guinea. On 23 November 1965, he called Hill in and gave him a typed, unsigned note. By handing Hill an informal note rather than a signed letter to the Australian government under the UNHCR letterhead, Schnyder indicated that he was trying to bend over backwards to accommodate Australian sensitivities. He assured Hill that his approach had not been "prompted by his having received information in any way critical of the Australian Governments [*sic*] action" in relation to border crossers, and that "any information [the Australian government] might give him would be treated as entirely confidential, that it would not be distributed either within or outside his headquarters."[18] In the note, the High Commissioner told the Australians that they need not be afraid of involving the UNHCR:

> UNHCR would greatly appreciate the receipt of information on the procedures applied to persons belonging to the group in question seeking asylum in the Territory. Such information, as well as information relevant to the number of persons who have sought and who have been granted asylum, would be treated by UNHCR as of a confidential nature to the extent that such treatment would be considered necessary by the Australian government.[19]

The note did not request the UNHCR's involvement in the refugee determination process, nor a visit by a UNHCR envoy to the Australian Territory.

By the time the Australians had agreed on a response to the High Commissioner's request, Schnyder had been replaced by Prince Sadruddin Aga Khan. In January 1966, Hill formally briefed Sadruddin, repeating the Australian line that the great majority of the border crossers "in no sense can be regarded as refugees." While Sadruddin agreed that he would treat all information provided by the Australian government about the refugee issue in New Guinea as confidential, he was far more assertive than his predecessor. He told Hill that "while he had no reason to complain in respect of any decisions taken so far by the authorities in Papua and New Guinea, it was his responsibility to ensure that the cases of asylum seekers were given full consideration."[20]

Schnyder kept quiet about the West Papuan refugees because he tried to accommodate the interests of the Australian government. Sadruddin's reluctance to draw attention to the issue was also informed by his attitude towards Indonesia. In October 1965, the military under Suharto had deposed President Sukarno. The coup was accompanied by an anti-communist purge and by racial violence against Indonesia's Chinese minority. About half a million people were killed. On that occasion, Sadruddin decided that the UNHCR's intervention would amount to interference in the domestic affairs of a sovereign state, and remained silent about the bloodshed and the mass displacements in Indonesia.[21] The Indonesian government was as interested as its Australian counterpart in sidelining the UNHCR over the refugee issue in New Guinea. Having accommodated the interests of the Suharto government in the aftermath of the coup, it made little sense for Sadruddin then to offend Suharto by insisting on the UNHCR's involvement in New Guinea.

Yet under Sadruddin, the office of the UNHCR developed serious misgivings about aspects of the Australian response to West Papuan refugees. In 1968, for example, the UNHCR's legal adviser, Arnold Rørholt, queried the Australian practice of having patrol officers make decisions on the spot about whether or not border crossers were genuine refugees. He also queried the fact that those who were not deemed to be genuine refugees had no right of appeal.[22] Sadruddin himself often demanded that the Australian representative in Geneva respond to claims made by West Papuans living in exile or to media reports. He also repeatedly suggested that a UNHCR representative visit Papua and New Guinea to gain a first-hand impression of the refugee question.

Such a visit, however, was anathema to the Australian government. When Australia declined to sign the Bellagio Protocol, it did so partly because Article 2 of the Protocol obliged signatories to cooperate with the office of the High Commissioner in the exercise of its functions and in particular to facilitate the office's duty of supervising the application of the Protocol. Australia was alarmed at the prospect that a UNHCR representative would meddle in its affairs in Papua and New Guinea and in its delicate relationship with Indonesia. Commenting on the implications of the Protocol for the West Papuan refugee question, the Department of External Affairs legal adviser, Pat Brazil, wrote:

> It seems to me that... it might be very difficult in practice to maintain that the High Commissioner should not send a representative to the territory if his own opinion was that this was necessary.[23]

Until the granting of self-governance to Papua New Guinea in 1973, the Australian government successfully managed to keep the UNHCR effectively out of the territory, and to deal with the border crossers entirely on Australia's own terms. The Australian government frequently claimed that these terms were identical with those promoted by the UNHCR. In 1970, the government instructed the Administrator to tell the House of Assembly in Port Moresby that "the granting of permissive residence in the Territory to West Irians is dependent upon the principles laid down in the Convention Relating to the Status of Refugees."[24] But given Australia's unwillingness to sign the Protocol, such statements were largely rhetorical. Testament to Australia's and Indonesia's success in keeping the UNHCR sidelined is the fact that Louise Holborn's 1500-page history of the organisation (which was initiated by Sadruddin in the late 1960s) does not once mention West Papuan refugees.[25]

CHAPTER 7

Deportees

As seen in Chapter 2, Australia resettled a large number of refugees in the two decades following the second world war, both in absolute terms and by comparison with other countries. They were admitted for permanent residence and not expected to return to their countries of origin – even if such a return were considered safe owing to a change of political circumstances. Immigration authorities believed Australia was making an investment when it selected refugees for resettlement, and that it would lose out on its return if the new settlers stayed only temporarily.

Indeed, throughout Australia's history of settling refugees they have typically applied from overseas for admission to Australia, been selected by the immigration authorities, and then been granted permanent residence. There have been, however, important exceptions. In several instances, Australia admitted or tolerated refugees on the understanding that their stay would be temporary. Mostly this occurred after this book's cut-off date of 1973: the admission of East Timorese between 1975 and 1999; the – initially temporary – admission of Vietnamese evacuees in 1975; the granting of temporary visas to Chinese students in the wake of the Tiananmen Square massacre in 1989; the airlifting of Kosovars to Australia in 1999; and the issuing of temporary protection visas to asylum seekers who have been recognised as Convention refugees.

Some of the exceptions, though, did occur before 1973. As previously mentioned, during the second world war Australia admitted a small number of Polish refugees who had become stranded in Japan, on a temporary basis. Once the war was over, Australia did not insist on their repatriation.

Also during the second world war, on a much larger scale, 5473 non-Europeans, as well as about twice as many Europeans, arrived in Australia from Asia and the South Pacific as evacuees or refugees, and were permitted to remain for the duration of the war. These included seamen who were allowed to seek work onshore – for example, because their ship was requisitioned by the Australian navy. After the war, Arthur Calwell was determined to repatriate the non-European wartime refugees as soon as shipping capacities permitted. Most of them were anxious to return home. But some were reluctant to leave because they had married an Australian, had Australian-born children, or had found work opportunities that were not available at home.

Calwell backed up his stance by referring to statements the government had made during the war. When entering Australia, the non-European evacuees and refugees had known that their stay would only be for the duration of the hostilities in the Pacific. The government had made no promises that temporary entrants would eventually be granted permanent residence status. Some of them had at the time acknowledged in writing that their stay in Australia would only be temporary. Samad Abdul bin Amjah, for example, who had arrived in Brisbane in 1943 as a sailor on the MV *Gorgon*, told the Australian authorities when requesting permission to work onshore:

> As I have experienced some hardships during the war, been bombed and been in hospitals with wounds from bomb splinters, and also been in hospital recently with an attack of Malaria Fever, I feel I would like to have a rest on shore for a while... I do not intend to settle down in Australia, as I have got my home with my mother, sister and brothers in Malacca, to where I intend to return as soon as the war is over.[1]

Once Amjah had married an Australian and had Australian-born children, he naturally changed his mind. But for the Department of the Interior, and, after 1945, the Department of Immigration, the depth of attachments that non-European wartime refugees formed in Australia – be it through relationships with Australians, or through their employment – had no bearing on their residence status. The extent to which they had made a contribution to Australia also had no impact on the immigration department's stance – Amjah, for instance, had served in the Australian merchant navy and been wounded in Milne Bay.

At the time, the public usually approved of Australia's restricted immigration policy. But Calwell's uncompromising stance met with little sympathy when it affected Australians of European ancestry who were married to non-European wartime refugees faced with deportation. Their cases received sympathetic treatment in the press, and their appeals to the minister were supported by many Australians who could not understand why the letter of the law had to be applied to non-Europeans whose conduct had been exemplary. Two cases, in particular, caught the public imagination in the late 1940s: that of Amjah and thirteen other Malay seamen, all of them married to Australians, who were deported on the SS *Marella* to Singapore in December 1947; and the attempted deportation in 1949 of Annie O'Keefe, an Ambonese wartime refugee married to an Australian.

In both cases, the immigration department was successfully challenged in the Australian courts. In Amjah's case, the successful court action did not occur before his original deportation but after he had returned by jumping ship in Sydney and then been threatened with deportation again. For O'Keefe, it was the delay between her entry and her proposed deportation that led to a successful court challenge. Like other wartime evacuees, O'Keefe had entered Australia as a refugee and had neither been required to sit a dictation test, nor been issued with a certificate of exemption. The High Court ruled that, five years after her arrival, she could not be declared a prohibited immigrant by making her sit, and fail, a dictation test.[2] In response to that decision, the Labor government rushed the Wartime Refugees Removal Act through parliament. The Act enabled the Department of Immigration to deport wartime refugees regardless of the circumstances under which they had been admitted.

The Act came into force in July 1949, some six months before the Labor government was voted out of office. Despite Calwell's determination to use the Act to rid Australia of the "recalcitrant minority" of non-European wartime refugees[3] the Act had little effect, either before the elections (because the immigration department deferred the serving of deportation orders), or afterwards (because Calwell's successor, Harold Holt, allowed the remaining wartime refugees to stay in Australia).

The cases involving Chinese who were allowed to remain in Australia although, technically, they could have been deported are closely related to those of the wartime refugees. In the 1950s, there were about 600 Chinese temporary entrants, many of them students, who were unwilling to return home after the fall of mainland China to the communists in 1949. The Menzies government granted them residence permits under the so-called Liberal Attitude Status policy, in a decision similar to Prime Minister Bob Hawke's after the 1989 Tiananmen Square massacre. Of course, neither the Chinese who had entered Australia on temporary visas before 1949 nor those who had come as students before June 1989 had arrived as refugees.

West Papuan refugees were another group who could have been deported, but were not. In the 1960s and 1970s, Australia granted temporary permissive residence visas to hundreds of West Papuan refugees in the Australian Territory of Papua and New Guinea (see Chapter 5). These visas were routinely renewed. In December 1971, for example, all permits were extended until 31 December 1973.[4] For years, many West Papuan refugees could never be certain whether or not they would be allowed to remain in the Territory of Papua and New Guinea, but I have not found evidence of a single case in which a permissive resident was told to return to West Irian/Irian Jaya after the expiry of her or his permit.

•

While resettlement has been the Australian government's desired outcome where refugees were recruited as immigrants, permanent residence status has always been a privilege rather than a right. Even the displaced persons (DPs) resettled under the auspices of the International Refugee Organisation (IRO) were not automatically granted permanent residence permits but had to earn that privilege by fulfilling two-year work contracts.

And for successive Australian governments, the granting of that right to permanent residence, and the repatriation of non-citizens whose temporary permits had expired, were separate issues. The Liberal Attitude Status policy reflected Australia's reluctance to repatriate long-term residents to the People's Republic of China and also its difficulty in obtaining re-entry documents from the Chinese government, with whom Australia had no diplomatic relations. But the policy did not automatically confer permanent residence status on those affected by it. The government would have happily sent Chinese temporary visa holders elsewhere, if it had found an Asian country willing to take them.

It would seem reasonable to assume that the government's reluctance to deport people to the People's Republic of China was the result of humanitarian considerations. Yet, more widely, the question of whether or not deportees would be persecuted after their return was not foremost in the minds of those formulating and administering Australia's immigration policy, as the following examples show.

In September 1946, while leading a patrol in Papua's Western District, D. R. Marsh encountered several bands of Javanese seeking refuge in the Australian Territory. One group, comprising 38 men, handed him a letter in Malay. The Australian administration's translation reads:

> We are refugees from Merauke Dutch Territory for we are Indonesians from Java. [We] refuse to work with the Dutch Government for fighting our country Republic Indonesia. The Dutch Government will not allow us to return to Java, therefore we take this way to look for protection of Australian Commonwealth.[5]

Marsh noted that the Javanese had been delighted to meet an Australian representative and see the Australian flag, and that theirs was a "pitiful story." Nevertheless, he sent all of them back to Dutch territory. In fact, he would have handed them over to the West New Guinean authorities, had a Dutch patrol met him as arranged.[6]

Over the following months, the government's policy towards Indonesia shifted, with Australia siding more openly with the Indonesian nationalists against the Dutch. Three months after Marsh's encounters with Javanese refugees in Papua, the Australians detained seven Indonesians in New Guinea's Sepik District, who claimed to be escaped political prisoners. This time, the government decided that they should not be returned to Dutch New Guinea but instead "treated as prohibited immigrants" and "deported from New Guinea to an Indonesian controlled port in Java."[7]

Once it had decided to support the Indonesian nationalist cause, the government went to extraordinary lengths to ensure that the Dutch would not be able to seize deportees from Papua and New Guinea. In May 1947, Soegoro Atmaprasaja, one of the leaders of the Indonesian independence movement in Dutch New Guinea, arrived in Daru, in Papua's Western District, after escaping from a Dutch prison. In November, the Australian government flew him to Darwin to join other Indonesians who were being repatriated to Indonesian-controlled territory courtesy of the Australian air force. As the Dutch refused to rule out arresting Soegoro during a refuelling stop in Soerabaya, the Australians prevented him from boarding the plane.

For more than a year, he remained in Darwin at the government's expense, even though the Northern Territory's Administrator accused him of stirring up the local indigenous people. The authorities were clearly anxious to see the last of Soegoro, whose propaganda they believed to be potentially dangerous, particularly if disseminated among Papua New Guineans or Aborigines.[8] But they did not compromise his safety, and tolerated his presence until December 1948, when an agreement with the Indian high commissioner made it possible for Soegoro to return to Indonesian territory via India – a route which Tasman Heyes considered, oddly enough, "the quickest and cheapest method ensuring his leaving Australia."[9]

Throughout the period surveyed in this book – from the late 1930s to the early 1970s – the Australian authorities tried to avoid deporting people to countries whose governments Australia opposed. During the Cold War, the government's unwillingness to deport non-citizens to communist countries even resulted in Australia's harbouring Eastern European war criminals. Australia's policy depended not so much on whether or not a deportee would face persecution, as on whether Australia was on friendly terms with the regime persecuting him or her. In 1962, Garfield Barwick wanted to deport the three Portuguese asylum seekers from the *Goncalves Zarco* to Portugal because that country was Britain's oldest ally – regardless of the Salazar regime's notoriety for human rights violations (see Chapter 4). The government returned West Papuan border crossers less because of the treatment they might receive at the hands of the Indonesian security forces, than because of Australia's relationship with Indonesia.

•

Australian reservations about deportations to China gradually mounted during the 1950s. Chinese nationals comprised a large contingent of those Australia deported: in 1951–52, 35 of 422 deportees were Chinese; the following year, the proportion was even higher with 44 out of 251.[10] Chinese deportees included residents who had been convicted of criminal offences, who had engaged in prostitution, or who were illegal immigrants. The latter were either ship's deserters or stowaways. Since federation, Australia's immigration authorities had been very concerned about Chinese who entered Australia as stowaways aided by people smugglers. The government regarded deportation as a means of discouraging both prospective illegal immigrants and those organising their entry.

In the early 1950s, Australia regularly sent Chinese deportees to Hong Kong, and then relied on the crown colony's authorities to escort them across the Chinese border. This sometimes involved force, as the following excerpt from a 1953 memorandum, about the immigration department's handling of deportation to China, demonstrates:

> The master on the last voyage had to keep the deportee on board for 48 hours before the escort came to take him over the border and the escort then had to clout him over the head to quieten him before they could handcuff him.[11]

In 1955, the government of Formosa (Taiwan) indicated that it would admit Chinese deportees to save them from being persecuted in China, but failed to make a concrete offer to Australia. In 1959, Alexander Downer decided to stop deporting deserters who hailed from mainland China if they had lived in Australia for at least five years. Chinese stowaways, however, continued to be deported to Hong Kong from where they were escorted across the border to the People's Republic.

Deportations to China became a major political issue in 1962. On 12 April, the head of the immigration department, Peter Heydon, noted in his diary: "A great hullabaloo developed in the late afternoon promoted by Kent Hughes and Wentworth about the deportation of a Chinese stowaway to mainland China."[12] The "hullabaloo" concerned an illegal immigrant, Willie Wong (aka Billy Wong or Bee Lee Wong), who had been detained after an immigration officer had found him working without papers in a market garden in Matraville (Sydney). Wong claimed that he had left China for Hong Kong in 1954, and stowed away to Australia that same year. Liberal parliamentarian Wilfrid Kent Hughes intervened on behalf of Wong, but by the time the minister, Alexander Downer, told his parliamentary colleague that the matter was being investigated, Wong was already on a ship bound for Hong Kong. Kent Hughes and fellow Liberal backbencher Bill Wentworth were furious when they found out that Wong was about to be escorted across the border, and threatened to deprive the government of its majority in the House of Representatives. To placate the two government parliamentarians and published opinion, the immigration department tried to intercept Wong on his way to the border, but failed.[13]

On this occasion, most Australian newspapers, and the press in Malaya and Hong Kong, were highly critical of the Australian practice of returning deportees to China. The Melbourne *Herald* carried a correspondent's report which purported to describe Wong's arrival at the Chinese border:

> On Wednesday, unhappy, bewildered, apprehensive and apologising to his Chinese police "escort," bowing respectfully to sympathetic English police officers at the border, he was transferred across the "no man's land" bridge at Lowu, to waiting armed Chinese Communist guards.[14]

Willie Wong's deportation came at a time when Western nations were under pressure to resettle Chinese refugees living in Hong Kong, as the crown colony's capacity to accommodate them was seemingly exhausted. In Australia, the Wong case provided the catalyst for a moratorium on deportations to China. It benefited other illegal immigrants from China who were awaiting their deportation at Sydney's

North Head quarantine station, which also functioned as an immigration detention centre. They included Wong Fun Cheung who, like Willie Wong, had come to Australia as a stowaway, and who had applied through his lawyer for political asylum (see Introduction).

•

In 1950, the Department of Immigration objected to the draft Refugee Convention in part because it would have prevented Australia from deporting refugees unless they threatened national security or public order. But neither Samad bin Amjah nor Willie Wong was a refugee in the sense of the 1951 Convention. Their deportations did not violate international law. Nor would they have, if Australia had acceded to the Convention without reservations.

So far, Australia has not deported people who have entered the country without a visa, applied for asylum, been formally recognised as Convention refugees, and been issued with a temporary protection visa. It is therefore often assumed that the deportation of somebody whose temporary protection visa has not been renewed would break new ground. But previous governments did deport immigrants whose status as refugees was undisputed – some before and some after the Convention was in place. Of the 843 DPs who arrived on the *General Stuart Heintzelman* in November 1947, four were immediately returned to Europe for health or security reasons.[15] David Dutton's research has shown that in the early 1950s, Australia deported some immigrants brought to Australia under the auspices of the IRO because they were found to be communists or fascists.[16] Others were deported because of criminal convictions. Such deportations were justifiable under the Refugee Convention.

But Australia also deported immigrants, including refugees, for "character" or medical reasons. In June 1950 the Minister for Immigration signed deportation orders for two Polish IRO-sponsored immigrants who had arrived six months earlier from Lebanon, on account of their "history of homosexuality."[17] Others were deported because of mental illness. The immigration department does not seem to have kept separate statistics about deported refugees. Thus we do not know how many of the 297 mentally or physically ill persons deported from Australia between 1950 and 1962 had originally entered the country as refugees.[18] Most deportations for "character," health or security reasons appear to have happened in the first half of the 1950s, before Australia ratified the Convention. In 1963, Peter Heydon noted that since Australia's accession to the Convention in 1954, "there has not been any case in which the Minister has deported a refugee on the ground that within five years after his arrival in Australia 'he has become an inmate of an insane asylum or public charitable institution'."[19]

There is at least one later case in which a mentally ill refugee was removed from Australian territory. Adrian Dedda was a West Papuan medical student whom the Dutch had sponsored to study in Port Moresby. After the Dutch left West New Guinea, he refused to return home and applied for political asylum in Papua and New Guinea. Dedda was politically active in Port Moresby – he contributed to the anti-Indonesian newsletter *Eastern Voice* – and had reason to fear the Indonesian authorities. Allowed to remain in the Australian Territory, he graduated in 1965 and commenced work in a Port Moresby hospital. Subsequently, he became mentally ill – claiming, for instance, that he was the illegitimate son of General MacArthur – and was admitted to a mental institution. The Director of Public Health considered Dedda certifiable; the Territory's administration, however, did not consider it advisable to certify him except in the event that he contacted the media to draw attention to his case.[20]

In October 1967, the Department of External Affairs informed the Indonesian government that Dedda "has expressed a wish to return to West Irian and our Embassy is seeking the assistance of the Department of Foreign Affairs in returning him to Sukarnapura where we understand there are good facilities for the treatment of mental illness."[21] Strictly speaking, of course, Dedda was not deported. But whether or not he requested his repatriation is irrelevant, as the Australian authorities themselves were convinced that Dedda no longer understood what he was talking about. When representing the case to the Australian media, however, a letter from Dedda was a convenient excuse, and the Department of Territories was anxious not to delay the repatriation "in case Dedda writes again in different vein."[22]

On 4 December 1967, Dedda and a West Papuan refugee who had a criminal record were flown back to West Irian, accompanied by

Superintendent Purcell from the Territory's Corrective Institutions Branch. A subsequent report noted:

> [T]he party was met at the Sentani airport by a group of 12 West Irian officials comprised of 6 Police Inspectors... 2 Indonesian Migration officials and 2 Indonesian civilian officials who were probably medical authorities but may have been security personnel... Dr. Dedda was taken outside the reception building and Superintendent Purcell was under the impression that he was to be vaccinated... No indication as to [his] future was given by the Indonesian officials.[23]

I could find no documentation to suggest that the Australian government attempted to ascertain what happened to Dedda after his return.

During Philip Ruddock's tenure as Minister for Immigration (1996–2003), Australia deported several asylum seekers who seemed to have a reasonable case for seeking Australia's protection but did not meet the Convention's historically contingent criteria. In June 2002, an Iranian man, Nadar Sayadi-Estahbanati, was forcibly deported after he had exhausted all legal avenues to challenge the immigration department's decision not to recognise him as a refugee. Together with his brother Nasser and another man, Nadar Sayadi-Estahbanati had arrived in Portland, Victoria, as a stowaway in 2000 aboard an Iranian ship. Nasser Sayadi-Estahbanati voluntarily returned to Iran after failing in his attempt to obtain refugee status, and disappeared on the day of his arrival. Ruddock authorised Nadar Sayadi-Estahbanati's deportation despite grave concerns by refugee advocates about the deportee's physical and mental health, and about the prospect that he would meet the same fate as his brother. In his last contact with a friend in Melbourne, Nadar Sayadi-Estahbanati said that he had been interrogated for several days on his return.[24] Labor's Carmen Lawrence raised the issue of his deportation on several occasions in parliament, but was not able to ascertain his fate after his arrival in Iran.[25]

There were comparable incidents well before the current collective angst about "boat people." They concerned individuals who could not demonstrate they had suffered or would suffer from politically motivated persecution, such as the hundreds of West Papuan "non-political native refugees" referred to in Chapter 5. In 1948, Australia repatriated two West Papuans to Dutch New Guinea who had assisted Soegoro Atmaprasaja after his escape from a Dutch prison and accompanied him across the border. Soegoro had maintained that all three would be imprisoned if handed over to the Dutch. But as the Dutch were not going to charge the two West Papuans with a "political" offence but instead with "aiding an escaped prisoner" and "horse stealing," the Australian authorities saw no reason to grant them asylum.[26]

As the cases in this chapter have shown, Australian authorities opted for deportation (or repatriation – the distinction often being only technical) for two main reasons: to deter particular groups of would-be immigrants, and to remove a person whose continued presence was regarded as a liability. The former applied in the cases of Chinese stowaways and West Papuan border crossers. The latter was a consideration in the case of Dedda (whose continued presence was thought to potentially embarrass the Australian Territory's administration), and in the cases of mentally ill refugees. The deportation of a refugee on the grounds that he or she had been admitted to a psychiatric institution highlights the congruence of the government's refugee policy with its immigration policy.

When, however, the government opted against the instrument of deportation, it tended to be for ideological reasons. During the Cold War, it was therefore most reluctant to authorise deportations to Soviet bloc countries. The fate potentially befalling a deportee upon his or her return mattered far less to the decision-makers than the government's opposition to the communist regime in question. The prospect of adverse publicity in Australia was another important consideration. The repatriation of Amjah and the other Malay seamen in 1947, Annie O'Keefe's attempted deportation some eighteen months later, the case of the three Portuguese sailors, and Wong's deportation in 1962 became causes célèbres that excited Australian public opinion – far more than the deportation of Sayadi-Estahbanati in 2002. Whether or not Wong and other Chinese deportees would really have been taken into custody by "armed Chinese Communist guards," as the *Herald*'s correspondent suggested, mattered only once the issue had been made public.

Publicly, neither Barwick (in the case of the three Portuguese sailors) nor Downer (in the case of Wong) discounted the humanitarian argument put forward in newspaper editorials. Barwick reversed an earlier decision to deport the Portuguese asylum seekers, and Downer would have reversed his decision to deport Wong if it had been possible to intercept him in Hong Kong. Publicly, in the first three postwar decades, only Calwell – like Ruddock more than half a century later – claimed that the humanitarian argument should not be accorded first priority. Calwell – and Ruddock – argued that even in the case of refugees the integrity of Australia's immigration policy was more important than any humanitarian considerations.

Conclusion

Did Australia react as an exemplary international citizen to the various refugee crises between the late 1930s and the early 1970s? Did it respond generously to individuals seeking its protection? A close look at the historical evidence in the preceding chapters has largely answered these questions in the negative.

The admission of refugees peaked in the late 1940s and early 1950s. Australia resettled 182,159 refugees alone under the auspices of the International Refugee Organisation (IRO), more than any other country except the United States. But in order to appreciate such figures, one ought to be aware of why Australia welcomed European displaced persons (DPs) and refugees sponsored by the IRO. Australia tried to attract as many of "those good people" as possible, because the Chifley and Menzies governments believed that Australia needed to significantly increase its population and thus its migrant intake, because British migrants were not available in sufficient numbers, and because the IRO provided transport at a time when shipping capacities were scarce.

Australia's motivation in itself should not detract from its contribution. But its rationale for resettling refugees determined the way it selected them. In the late 1940s and early 1950s, Australia recruited refugees who met its requirements, rather than admitted refugees on the basis of their individual needs. DPs were selected with a view to increase Australia's pool of labour. Claims that Australia was traditionally generous in its refugee intake are disingenuous if the high number of admissions of DPs under the IRO scheme is cited as key supporting evidence.

Even in numerical terms, Australia's acceptance of refugees was less generous at other, less convenient times. Australia admitted far fewer refugees fleeing Europe as a result of the policies of Nazi Germany than it might have. Australia was the last traditional resettlement country to confine its refugee intake to those of European ancestry and appearance. When Idi Amin expelled Uganda's Asians, Australia resettled only a comparatively small contingent of expellees, most of whom were selected under the immigration department's non-European policy on account of their skills and qualifications.

Instances in which Australia resettled refugees regardless of whether or not they were suitable immigrants are comparatively rare. They include the largely uncontrolled (and, at the time, highly controversial) immigration of Jewish survivors immediately after the second world war, and the resettlement of European refugees with a disability in the early 1960s in the wake of World Refugee Year.

In 1954, Australia was only the sixth nation to accede to the 1951 Convention Relating to the Status of Refugees. It has played a prominent role in international organisations set up to provide relief to refugees: the United Nations Relief and Rehabilitation Administration (UNRRA), the IRO and the United Nations High Commissioner for Refugees (UNHCR). But when ratifying the Refugee Convention, Australia made reservations to key articles and elected to limit its scope to people who had become refugees as a result of events taking place before 1951 in Europe. Australia did not sign the 1967 Protocol, which removed the Convention's geographical and time limitations, until 1973. In the early 1950s, Australia collaborated with the United States and other traditional migrant receiving countries in setting up the Intergovernmental Committee for European Migration in direct competition with the UNHCR.

Australia's current policies have precedents. In the 1960s, it refused refuge to many West Papuans without properly investigating whether or not their asylum claims were well-founded. It repatriated and deported refugees in the past, including some whose refugee status was not in dispute. Similarly, the current hostility towards asylum seekers in published and public opinion and among Australia's elected representatives has historical parallels. In the immediate postwar years, newspaper editorials warned against the admission of Jewish survivors. In the early 1970s, the McMahon government refused to accept more than a handful of expellees from Uganda, not least because it was concerned a generous offer would jeopardise its chances of winning the 1972 elections (which it lost anyway). Occasional interventions by mavericks such as the Liberals' Wilfrid Kent Hughes or Labor's Jim Cairns aside, Australia's self-interested refugee policies always had bipartisan support in the House of Representatives.

Between the 1930s and the early 1970s – that is, before Australia incurred obligations towards non-European refugees under international law – Australia was not particularly generous, either in its acceptance of refugees, or in its support for the UNHCR and the principles of the 1951 Convention, or when deciding whether or not to remove asylum seekers and other non-citizens. The evocation of a golden age when Australians welcomed those fleeing persecution and their government played a key role in alleviating the plight of refugees worldwide, is based on a selective, somewhat inaccurate reading of the past.

What could be gained from debunking widely held assumptions about Australian responses to refugees? Does it matter now whether or not Australia had an impeccable humanitarian record in the 1930s or in the 1960s? I believe that for six reasons, a history such as the one I have sketched in this book has a use beyond filling in a blank in Australian historiography.

First, a history attuned to the complexity of the past may make it more difficult for those debating current policies to make rhetorical references to the past in order to condemn or endorse the present. Australia's current response to the plight of refugees is neither the seamless continuation of a proud tradition, nor an aberration that could be criticised merely by invoking such a tradition. By gaining a better understanding of the past, we may be better able to criticise the present on its own terms (rather than in terms of supposed genealogies which only ever allow the past to have one outcome).

Second, a critical and nuanced history could prompt us to question the function of the past's rhetorical use in the present. When refugee advocacy groups invoke Australia's "traditional generosity,"[1] they appeal to Australians' nationalist sentiment. They suggest that the current government sullies the good name of Australia. I am wary of arguments that rely on a strong emotional identification with the nation – not least because such identification has historically provided a sound base for anti-alienism and collective egotism. When, on the other hand, the Department of Immigration invokes Australia's "proud record,"[2] it may do so to argue subtly for an exemption from Australia's responsibilities – much as Britain's *Daily Mail* editorialised in early 2003: "Britain has a proud tradition of sheltering the persecuted. But it has no moral or historical duty to be the world's favourite haven for everyone claiming asylum."[3]

Third, a history of Australian responses to refugees may help us gain a better sense of the legacies of the past in the present. (An interest in such legacies is distinct from a genealogical interest in that the former takes the past, the latter the present, as its point of departure.) In this book, I have highlighted one legacy, in particular: the formulation of refugee policies in the context of immigration policies. I have attempted to show how between the late 1930s and the early 1970s, the government's approach to refugees was always part of its broader approach to immigration. That changed to some extent from the 1970s onwards, as Australia developed a separate refugee policy and introduced a quota for the admission of refugees. But those administering a supposedly autonomous refugee policy were identical with those who had previously thought of refugees primarily as immigrants. The immigration department's "culture of control'[4] has arguably shaped official Australian responses to refugees until now. An analysis of the explicit subsumption of refugee policy under immigration policy until the 1970s may enable us to recognise – and question – the implicit expectation after the 1970s that refugee policy be subservient to immigration policy.

Fourth, history allows us not to take the present as a given. In John Howard's Australia, many of its citizens have come to accept that the government draws on collective angst, indeed manipulates and fans this angst, in the pursuit of electoral gain. Previous governments recognised the dangers inherent in such an approach. Neither Joseph Lyons (in 1938 and 1939) nor Ben Chifley (in 1945 and 1946) amplified widely held fears about the immigration of Jewish refugees, or endorsed the concerns held by organisations such as the Australian Natives' Association to the extent that Howard and Ruddock have legitimised policies of Pauline Hanson's One Nation party.

Living in the early twenty-first century, it is also easy to forget that arguments informed by collective egotism have not always counted as much as arguments informed by, say, what Garfield Barwick in 1962 called "traditional British principles." Refugee advocates arguing for a humanitarian approach in the 1960s were listened to because the validity of their argument was recognised – however grudgingly – even by those who wanted policy to be guided by other considerations. This is of course not to say that previous governments followed the humanitarian argument.

Fifth, the appreciation of a past that is markedly different from the present may allow us to imagine solutions beyond the straightjacket of the status quo. Between 1945 and 1948, the Australian government moved first to create a department solely concerned with the implementation of its immigration policy (namely, the Department of Immigration), and then authorised the new department to recruit up to 200,000 IRO-sponsored migrants in Europe. Notwithstanding the motivation behind the large-scale recruitment of refugees, it was a visionary approach to Australia's perceived need to increase its population.

While Calwell's vision was for a Greater White Australia rather than for a solution to the European refugee crisis, his ambition to increase Australia's population made a significant contribution to alleviating the plight of Europe's DPs. Visionary politics, whatever their aim, are as notably absent from current debates in parliament as they are from the public discourse on refugee policies. Does not the scope of today's global refugee crisis call for a response as bold as Calwell's approach to the IRO in the late 1940s? Would not incremental reform (such as the replacement of mandatory detention by a detention regime that spares children) merely mitigate and thereby confirm the status quo? Over a twelve-month period in 1949–50, Australia, with a population of hardly more than a third of today's, accommodated some 100,000 DPs and refugees at a time when the country, and the majority of its citizens, were not nearly as affluent as they are today.

Let us imagine an equivalent of Australia's postwar immigration programme that is bold enough to send a signal to those living in the privileged corners of this world – as bold, say, as Norway's commitment to meet a target set in 1958 by the World Council of Churches and spend 1 per cent of its GNP on foreign aid. Could Australia afford to provide not 4376 places under its refugee programme (as it did in 2002–03) but ten times as many in a gesture designed not only to impress the rest of the world but, more importantly, to challenge Australians to collectively enact qualities that are supposedly part of their national character? Could Australia not afford a general amnesty for illegal immigrants and a gesture that granted permanent residence status to all asylum seekers who are now in Australia or its off-shore prison on Nauru?

The establishment of a separate Department of Immigration was central to the mass immigration programme envisaged by the Chifley government. The department dealt with refugees by default. Curtin, Chifley and Calwell could not have foreseen that refugees would comprise a large proportion of Australia's migrant intake in the late 1940s and throughout the 1950s. The establishment of a separate government agency responsible for the administration of Australia's refugee policy is long overdue. Admittedly, that would be as bold a move as the excision of the immigration functions from the Department of the Interior in 1945.

This proposal may sound anachronistic at a time when it seems increasingly difficult to distinguish between refugees and economic migrants. This difficulty, however, has not arisen because migrants now routinely masquerade as refugees, but because they are increasingly forced to leave their homes for reasons that include, among others, those listed in Article 1 of the 1951 Refugee Convention. By establishing an agency responsible for refugee assistance, the government would acknowledge that it has a responsibility towards people who emigrate because the push factor (forced displacement) far outweighs the pull factor (the attractiveness of prospective resettlement countries), and that this responsibility is not affected by the requirements of Australia's immigration programme.

Sixth, history may offer us a roundabout way of addressing issues that are routinely put in the too-hard basket. Prominent among those is the question of why Australia should assist refugees, be it by generously funding programmes that deal with the root causes of forced displacement or by admitting refugees for resettlement. Historically, policy makers have been guided by a combination of five factors: (i) international legal obligations; (ii) domestic pressure; (iii) national (self-)interest; (iv) international reputation; and (v) "humanitarian commitment and responsibility" (the first of four principles to guide Australia's refugee policy, which were announced by the Minister for Immigration, Michael McKellar, in 1977).[5]

For the period discussed in this book, we can discount the first factor. As Australia had ratified the Refugee Convention with a crucial caveat, and did not sign the Protocol until 1973, international law did not guide its refugee and asylum seeker policies before 1973.

Domestic public opinion in favour of refugees mattered only in exceptional instances, such as the case of the Portuguese sailors who sought asylum in 1961 and that of Samad bin Amjah and other wartime refugees married to Australians. In the second half of the 1940s, policy-makers paid attention to domestic public opinion averse to the admission of refugees, when they restricted the admission of Jewish refugees and carefully selected the first shipload of IRO-sponsored DPs to persuade the Australian public of their worthiness. In the early 1970s, the McMahon government supposedly objected to playing a more prominent role in the Ugandan relief effort because of the forthcoming elections. But in comparison to the early twenty-first century, successive governments from the 1930s to the 1970s were far more prepared to pursue policies regardless of the public's anticipated or initial reaction. I could find no instance in that earlier period in which the government encouraged public opinion against refugees.

National (self-)interest was the dominant factor influencing decisions to admit refugees. Australia wanted immigrants, and was prepared to accept refugees in lieu of British migrants as long as the former met its strict selection criteria. In times of economic downturn, the migrant intake (and, by implication, the refugee intake) were lowered. National (self-)interest was also the determining factor in decisions not to admit refugees. In the case of West Papuan border crossers, Australia was concerned it would damage its relationship with Indonesia if it adopted a more liberal attitude.

The argument that Australia's international reputation would suffer if the country did not respond more generously to a given refugee crisis was almost as ineffectual in the 1930s, 1940s, 1950s and 1960s as it has been in the early twenty-first century. Concerns about Australia's international standing mattered most between the late 1950s and early 1970s, when Australia was increasingly under attack over its White Australia policy, and in response often went to great lengths to demonstrate its credentials as a good international citizen. I do not know of any case before 1973, however, in which concerns about Australia's standing in the world overrode perceived national interests articulated by immigration or foreign policy.

Humanitarian considerations were not a major factor in the formulation and administration of refugee policies before 1973. Comparatively, they mattered most in the case of the West Papuan border crossers in the 1960s and 1970s. Australia was under no legal obligation to grant permissive residence visas to West Papuan refugees, and the government was under little external or domestic pressure to do so. It was arguably not in Australia's interest to admit West Papuans to the Australian Territory of Papua and New Guinea, however small their number: their presence had the potential to offend the Indonesians, and to create problems in a colony destined to become independent before too long. (It is perhaps not incidental that the Department of Immigration had almost no influence over asylum seeker policy in the Territory.)

A refugee policy that is divorced from immigration policy is potentially guided by humanitarian commitment and responsibility more so than by other factors. To approach the vexed question of how such commitment and responsibility ought to be defined, it may be useful to examine past Australian responses to refugees and asylum seekers with the benefit of hindsight. For example, did Australia have a responsibility towards West Papuan refugees because of its condoning of Indonesia's takeover of the former Dutch colony, or simply because of the situation they found themselves in?

This book has largely been about the policies and actions of the Australian government. It is not possible to measure Australia's generosity by evaluating only what its government did or failed to do. Australians have often been hostile to people they have labelled "reffos," "Balts" or "boat people." Only a small minority of Australians lobbied the government to admit Spanish refugees in 1939, to increase its quota for refugees from Nazi Germany, to accept refugees with a disability in the late 1950s, and to open its doors to Asian refugees from Hong Kong in 1962 and from Uganda ten years later. And most of those raising their voices on behalf of refugees did so because they believed it was the government's responsibility to assist refugees.

The Howard government's hardline approach to asylum seekers, in particular, is not unprecedented. What is unprecedented is the willingness of many ordinary Australians in the last few years to assist refugees and asylum seekers – to the extent that some of them are risking a hefty prison sentence by harbouring escapees from detention centres. They consider it their personal duty – as well as their government's – to assist fellow humans in distress, regardless of whether or not they are fellow citizens. And while the precise rationale for, and desirable extent of, Australia's humanitarian commitment and responsibility is an issue so difficult as to be intimidating, the issue of an individual's responsibility as a citizen of a globalised world is comparatively straightforward. In the last instance, it is also the more important one.

Notes

Introduction

1 A. J. P. Hall & Hall to Garfield Barwick, 18 May 1962, A1838 1477/2/208, National Archives of Australia.

2 Garfield Barwick, marginal note, 24 May 1962, on ibid.

3 A. J. P. Hall & Hall to Garfield Barwick, 18 May 1962, A1838 1477/2/208, National Archives of Australia.

4 A. R. Downer, Cabinet submission, 16 May 1962, A1838 1477/2/208, National Archives of Australia.

5 *Commonwealth Parliamentary Debates*, Representatives, vol. 35, 2 May 1962, p. 1818.

6 Intelligence Report, Page 5/71, 16 March 1971, A1838 3036/10/2 part 1, National Archives of Australia.

7 Administrator to Territories, 17 March 1971, A1838 3036/10/2 part 1, National Archives of Australia.

8 A. S. Amjah to Australian Commissioner for Malaya, 2 April 1948, A446 1963/43246, National Archives of Australia.

9 Cabinet minute, decision no. 275, 1 June 1966, A5841 192, National Archives of Australia.

10 K. H. Bailey to Secretary Immigration, 20 September 1949, A446 1963/43246, National Archives of Australia.

11 Charles Price, "Australia and Refugees 1921–1976," report commissioned by the National Population Council, May 1990.

Chapter 1: Reffos

1 S. D. Rutland, "Jewish Immigration 1881–1933," in *The Australian People: An Encyclopedia of the Nation, Its People and Their Origins*, ed. James Jupp, Cambridge: Cambridge University Press (2001), p. 531; B. Christa, "Russians," in *The Australian People*, p. 639; G. Cresciani, "Italian Immigrants 1920–1945," in *The Australian People*, pp. 500–5.

2 Andrew Markus, "Jewish Migration to Australia 1938–49," *Journal of Australian Studies*, no. 13 (1983), p. 18.

3 ibid., p. 19.

4 Quoted in Michael Blakeney, *Australia and the Jewish Refugees 1933–1948*, Sydney: Croom Helm Australia (1985), p. 46.

5 Quoted in Michael R. Marrus, *The Unwanted: European Refugees from the First World War Through the Cold War*, Philadelphia: Temple University Press (2002), p. 157.

6 *Proceedings of the Intergovernmental Committee, Evian, July 6th to 15th, 1938: Verbatim Record of the Plenary Meetings of the Committee: Resolutions and Reports* (1938), p. 20.

7 Michael Blakeney, *Australia and the Jewish Refugees 1933–1948*, Sydney: Croom Helm Australia (1985), pp. 51–52.

8 Bruce to Prime Minister, 21 November 1938, A433 1943/2/46, National Archives of Australia.

9 *Commonwealth Parliamentary Debates*, Representatives, vol. 158, 1 December 1938, p. 2535.

10 ibid.

11 ibid., p. 2536.

12 Paul R. Bartrop, "The Australian Government's 'Liberalisation' of Refugee Immigration Policy in 1938: Fact or Myth?," *Menorah*, vol. 2, no. 1 (1988), pp. 71 and 78.

13 Arthur Calwell, *Commonwealth Parliamentary Debates*, Representatives, vol. 190, 6 March 1947, p. 432.

14 Arthur Calwell, *Commonwealth Parliamentary Debates*, Representatives, vol. 190, 12 March 1947, p. 578.

15 Irving Abella and Harold Troper, *None Is Too Many: Canada and the Jews of Europe 1933–1948*, New York: Random House (1983).

16 Quoted in ibid., p. 64.

17 Quoted in ibid., p. 17.

18 J. A. Carrodus to Secretary Department of External Affairs, 28 June 1939, A981 REF 14 part 1, National Archives of Australia.

19 Arthur Calwell, *Commonwealth Parliamentary Debates*, Representatives, vol. 190, 12 March 1947, p. 578.

20 Secretary Australasian Council of Trade Unions to R. G. Menzies, 17 August 1939, A981 REF 14 part 1, National Archives of Australia.

21 "Answers to Questions Raised by the Council for Civil Liberties," appendix to J. A. Carrodus to Secretary Council for Civil Liberties, 24 February 1939, A981 REF 1, National Archives of Australia.

22 Emery Barcs, *Backyard of Mars: Memoirs of the "Reffo" Period in Australia*, Sydney: Wildcat Press (1980), chapter 1.

23 War Cabinet minute, agendum 130/1941, 9 April 1941, A5954 370/10, National Archives of Australia.

24 Quoted in Paul R. Bartrop, "'Not a Problem for Australia': The Kristallnacht

Viewed from the Commonwealth, November 1938," *Journal of the Australian Jewish Historical Society*, vol. 10, part 6 (1989), p. 493.

25 "Migrant Landing Restrictions," *Sydney Morning Herald*, 7 February 1939.

26 Prime Minister's Department to High Commissioner's Office, 9 November 1938, A981 REF 1, National Archives of Australia.

Chapter 2: Balts

1 "Extract Prime Minister's Policy Speech 26 October 1922," A461 D349/1/5 part 1, National Archives of Australia.

2 Arthur A. Calwell, *How Many Australians Tomorrow?*, Melbourne: Reed & Harris (1945), between pp. 18 and 19.

3 ibid., p. 66.

4 ibid., p. 53.

5 *Commonwealth Parliamentary Debates*, Representatives, vol. 184, 2 August 1945, p. 4911.

6 *Commonwealth Parliamentary Debates*, Representatives, vol. 184, 29 August 1945, pp. 4979–80.

7 Charles Price, "Australia and Refugees 1921–1976," report commissioned by the National Population Council, May 1990, p. 18.

8 "'Refuse' of Europe not Wanted Here," *Herald*, 28 January 1947; "A.N.A. Leader Attacks Selection of Immigrants," *Sun*, 18 March 1947.

9 Quoted in "Fewer Landing Permits for Refugees," *Sydney Morning Herald*, 23 January 1947.

10 "Statement by the Minister for Immigration," 8 July 1948, A6980 S250105, National Archives of Australia.

11 T. H. E. Heyes to Australian Mission Berlin, 26 July 1949, A434 1949/3/16408, National Archives of Australia.

12 "Statement by the Minister for Immigration," 19 August 1949, A434 1949/3/16408, National Archives of Australia.

13 J. S. Ergas, "Immigration of Displaced Persons to South America and Australia," n.d. (circa 1948), A6980 S250105, National Archives of Australia.

14 Louise W. Holborn, *The International Refugee Organization: A Specialized Agency of the United Nations: Its History and Work 1946–1952*, London: Oxford University Press (1956), pp. 407–8.

15 J. S. Ergas, "Immigration of Displaced Persons to South America and Australia," n.d. (circa 1948), A6980 S250105, National Archives of Australia.

16 J. V. Greenhalgh, "D.P. Migration Scheme – Operating Instruction No. 71," 19 June 1950, A6980 S250108, National Archives of Australia.

17 A. J. Metcalfe to Senior Medical Officer, 1 February 1949, A6980 S250106, National Archives of Australia.

18 E. F. Kunz, *Displaced Persons: Calwell's New Australians*, Sydney: Australian National University Press (1988), p. 38.

19 *Commonwealth Parliamentary Debates*, Representatives, vol. 207, 27 April 1950, pp. 1969–70.

20 Price, "Australia and Refugees," p. 28.

21 Athol Townley, *Commonwealth Parliamentary Debates*, Representatives, vol. 13, 8 November 1956, p. 2142.

22 Jockel to Tange, 22 December 1956, A10034 252/9/8-2, National Archives of Australia.

23 G. Jockel to A. H. Tange, 5 December 1956, A1838 33/2/6 part 1, National Archives of Australia.

24 Waterman to McKernan and Grant, 22 January 1957, A10034 252/9/8-2, National Archives of Australia.

25 Louise W. Holborn, *Refugees: A Problem of Our Time: The Work of the United Nations High Commissioner for Refugees, 1951–1972*, vol. 1, Methuchen: Scarecrow Press (1975), pp. 622 and 625.

26 T. H. E. Heyes to George Warren, 19 July 1957, A446 1962/67291, National Archives of Australia.

27 "Australia's contribution to the relief of the problem of refugees," 25 September 1959, A446 1962/67291, National Archives of Australia.

28 Price, "Australia and Refugees," pp. 30 and 48.

29 United Nations Information Service Geneva, press release no. REF/462, 20 February 1959, A10034 225/6-1, National Archives of Australia.

30 Price, "Australia and Refugees," p. 40.

31 Walter Nash, quoted in Anton Binzegger, *New Zealand's Policy on Refugees*, Wellington: New Zealand Institute of International Affairs (1980), p. 48.

32 I. D. Emerton to Assistant Secretary Planning & Research Division, 1 March 1960, A446 1965/46886, National Archives of Australia.

33 B. M. Martyn, file note, 17 May 1960, A446 1960/65417, National Archives of Australia.

34 "Press Statement by the Minister for Immigration: 250,000th Refugee Arrives Wednesday," 18 June 1960, A446 1960/65417, National Archives of Australia.

35 "Mr 250,000 (and Family) Looks Right at Home," *Sun*, 23 June 1960.

36 A. R. Lindt to Tasman Heyes, 14 June 1960, A446 1965/46886, National Archives of Australia.

37 A. L. Nutt to A. R. Lindt, 5 July 1960, A446 1965/46886, National Archives of Australia.

38 H. J. Murphy, "Publicity Needs in Australia for I.R.O. and Displaced Person Migrants," n.d. (1949), CP815/1 021.134, National Archives of Australia.

Chapter 3: Ineligibles

1 Gil Loescher, *The UNHCR and World Politics: A Perilous Path*, Oxford: Oxford University Press (2001), chapters 4 and 5; Mark Cutts (ed.), *The State of the World's Refugees: Fifty Years of Humanitarian Action*, Oxford: Oxford University Press (2000), chapters 1 and 2.

2 T. H. E. Heyes to Secretary Department of External Affairs, 22 November 1950, A1838 1531/1 part 1, National Archives of Australia.

3 Ralph Harry to Harold Grant, 20 February 1957, A1838 932/5/2 part 1, National Archives of Australia.

4 Australian High Commission Wellington to Department of External Affairs, 12 June 1962, A1838 932/5/3 part 1, National Archives of Australia.

5 "N. Z. Govt. Offer to Orphans Seen as Mistake," *Evening Post* (Wellington), 22 September 1962.

6 "Summary of Rules Generally Applying to Entry of Non-Europeans," 25 August 1966, A446 1966/45704, National Archives of Australia.

7 E. L. Charles, file note, 7 June 1967, A6980 S215059, National Archives of Australia.

8 John McCallum, *Commonwealth Parliamentary Debates*, Senate, vol. 21, 3 April 1962, p. 722.

9 Peter Heydon, diary, entry for 5 April 1962, MS3155 box 22, folder 184, National Library of Australia.

10 "Helping Kenyan Refugees," *Australian*, 10 March 1970.

11 Cabinet, decision no. 297, 30 April 1970, A446 1970/95188, National Archives of Australia.

12 Quoted in McGuiness for P. R. Heydon to Minister, 20 April 1970, A446 1970/95188, National Archives of Australia.

13 McGuiness for P. R. Heydon to Minister, 20 April 1970, A446 1970/95188, National Archives of Australia.

14 *Commonwealth Parliamentary Debates*, Representatives, vol. 79, 17 August 1972, p. 330.

15 Anthony Acland to Lord Bridges, 29 August 1972, appendix, PREM 15/1259, Public Record Office, London, quoted from digitised copy at <http://www.asiansfromuganda.org/1972/secret/secret.html>.

16 Downer to McMahon, 23 August 1972, A3211 1972/2790, National Archives of Australia.

17 Jenny S. Ellis to Alexander Downer, 15 September 1972, A3211 1972/2790, National Archives of Australia.

18 Alexander Downer to J. S. Ellis, 18 September 1972, A3211 1972/2790, National Archives of Australia.

19 *Commonwealth Parliamentary Debates*, Representatives, vol. 81, 17 October 1972, pp. 2741–42.

20 Alexander James Forbes, *Commonwealth Parliamentary Debates*, Representatives, vol. 81, 17 October 1972, p. 2742.

21 Immigration to Australian High Commission Nairobi, n.d. (27 September 1972), A5758 201/4/9/IU part 2, National Archives of Australia.

22 Department of Foreign Affairs, news release, M/11, 21 December 1972, Whitlam Institute (University of Western Sydney), <http://www.whitlam.org/collection/1972/1972_12_21_special_contribution.html>.

23 Prime Minister's Press Conference in London, 25 April 1973, Whitlam Institute (University of Western Sydney), <http://www.whitlam.org/collection/1973/19730425_PM_UK_Conference/>.

24 Al Grassby, *Commonwealth Parliamentary Debates*, Representatives, vol. 85, 27 September 1973, p. 1612.

25 Rodney Gouttman, "A Jew, and Coloured Too! Immigration of 'Jews of Middle East Origin' to Australia, 1949–58," *Immigrants and Minorities*, vol. 12, no. 1 (1993), pp. 75–91; Naomi Gale, "A Case of Double Rejection: The Immigration of Sephardim to Australia," *New Community*, vol. 20, no. 2, pp. 269–86.

26 G. V. Vance to Secretary, 18 February 1969, A1209 1969/7599, National Archives of Australia.

27 T. H. E. Heyes to Minister, 21 March 1957, A446 1970/95021, National Archives of Australia.

28 A. H. Borthwick to Secretary Department of External Affairs, memo no. 299, 5 April 1950, A1838 160/2/5/5, National Archives of Australia.

29 Cabinet minute, decision no. 481, 15 September 1964, A446 1970/95021, National Archives of Australia.

30 ibid.

31 W. K. Brown to Assistant Secretary Entry Policy Branch, 11 December 1968, A446 1970/95043, National Archives of Australia.

Chapter 4: Asylum seekers

1 *Commonwealth Parliamentary Debates*, Senate, vol. 42, 17 September 1969, p. 913.

2 ibid.

3 Heydon to Minister, 9 September 1969, A6980 S251033, National Archives of Australia.

4 Helen Frizell, "Law and the Refugee," *Sydney Morning Herald*, 22 February 1971.

5 "Statement by the Government Secretary, Mr. R. S. Leydin, Concerning Mrs. Petrov," 21 April 1954, A6122 11, National Archives of Australia.

6 Quoted in Robert Manne, *The Petrov Affair: Politics and Espionage*, Sydney: Pergamon (1987), p. 46.

7 ibid., p. 87.

8 Proceedings of Aliens Tribunal No. 4, 22 September 1941, p. 2, MP529/3 Tribunal 4/Huelscher, National Archives of Australia.

9 "Summary of personal particulars – Hulscher, Georg," n.d. (1940) MP529/2 Huelscher/G, National Archives of Australia.

10 Horgan to Collector of Customs Melbourne, 16 October 1936, B13 1936/24962, National Archives of Australia.

11 "Stowed Away for a Month," *Sydney Morning Herald*, 11 August 1941. I am grateful to Peter Browne for sourcing newspaper articles about Rozenberg's arrival in Australia.

12 L. Liveris to Secretary Immigration, 26 October 1956, E37 1978/10253, National Archives of Australia.

13 Cabinet, decision no. 487, 16 October 1956, A4926 398, National Archives of Australia.

14 ibid.

15 R. G. Casey, Cabinet submission no. 398, 4 October 1956, A4926 398, National Archives of Australia.

16 ibid.

17 C. C. F. Spry to Prime Minister, 10 October 1956, A1209 1957/4269, National Archives of Australia.

18 On Paranyuk's asylum case, see the following National Archives of Australia files: A1838 1606/3, A1209 1957/4351, and MP1139/1 V57/30023.

19 Anastasio Chamorro to Directors of Emmigration [*sic*], 9 November 1955, A10299 P12, National Archives of Australia.

20 Arthur Tange, marginal note on Patrick Shaw to Secretary, 1 December 1955, A1838 1522/47/783, National Archives of Australia.

21 Australian Embassy Washington to Department of External Affairs, 30 June 1959, A1209 1959/678, National Archives of Australia.

22 Department of External Affairs to Australian Embassy Washington, 6 July 1959, A1209 1959/678, National Archives of Australia.

23 Cabinet minute, Foreign Affairs and Defence Committee, 7 April 1965, A5928 854/FAD, National Archives of Australia; see also file A4940 C4166, National Archives of Australia.

24 Horgan, memorandum, 12 March 1945, A434 1946/3/10191, National Archives of Australia; Dusan Bojic, "The Half-Hearted Revolutionary in Paradise," *Lateline*, 22 September 2003, <http://www.abc.net.au/lateline/content/ 2003/hc40.htm>.

25 Douglas Lockwood, *The Front Door: Darwin, 1869–1969*, Adelaide: Rigby (1975), pp. 185–88.

26 P. R. Heydon to Minister for Immigration, 15 December 1961; A. H. Tange to Minister for External Affairs, 19 December 1961; both A446 1962/65208, National Archives of Australia.

27 H. G. Brooks to Secretary Immigration, 21 December 1961, A446 1962/65208, National Archives of Australia.

28 G. B. Feakes to Harry, 14 February 1962, A1838 49/2 part 1, National Archives of Australia.

29 Garfield Barwick, *A Radical Tory: Garfield Barwick's Reflections and Recollections*, Annandale: Federation Press (1995), p. 165.

30 E. L. Charles, "Notes of Discussions," 5 March 1962, A446 1962/65620, National Archives of Australia.

31 W. G. A. Landale, record of conversation between the Portuguese Chargé d'Affaires and the Minister for External Affairs on 6 March 1962; W. G. A. Landale, record of conversation between the Portuguese Chargé d'Affaires and the Minister for External Affairs on 20 March 1962; both A1838 1525/3/248 part 2, National Archives of Australia.

32 Barwick, *A Radical Tory*, p. 165.

33 W. G. A. Landale, record of conversation between the Portuguese Chargé d'Affaires and the Minister for External Affairs on 20 March 1962, A1838 1525/3/248 part 2, National Archives of Australia.

34 Peter Heydon diary, entry for 30 April 1962, MS3155 box 22, folder 184, National Library of Australia.

35 P. R. Heydon, "Note for Minister," 30 April 1962, A446 1962/65620, National Archives of Australia.

36 P. R. H[eydon] to Minister, n.d. (30 April 1962), A446 1962/65620, National Archives of Australia.

37 "Downer Felt Like Quitting," *Sunday Mirror*, 6 May 1962.

Chapter 5: Border crossers

1 Garfield Barwick, Cabinet submission no. 330, 19 July 1962, A1838 3036/14/1/6 part 1, National Archives of Australia.

2 "Meeting Held in Department of External Affairs on 6th August, 1964," A1838 3036/14/1/6 part 1, National Archives of Australia.

3 R. Marsh, "Policy regarding refugees from West New Guinea," 11 March 1964, A452 1963/8261, National Archives of Australia.

4 A. M. Bottrill to District Officer Wewak, 29 September 1964, A452 1964/229, National Archives of Australia.

5 Robert R. Cole to Secretary Department of the Administrator, 1 October 1964, A452 1964/229, National Archives of Australia.

6 Fredrik Mandowen, statement translated by J. Vandereit, 30 January 1964, A452 1963/8261, National Archives of Australia.

7 E. A. Simon, file note, 7 August 1964, A452 1963/8261, National Archives of Australia.

8 C. E. Barnes to B. H. Soer, 25 August 1964, A452 1963/8261, National Archives of Australia.

9 R. R. Cole to Secretary, Department of the Administrator, 28 September 1964, A452 1964/6361, National Archives of Australia.

10 Marsh to Minister, 23 November 1964; Barnes to Gorton, 9 December 1964; both A452 1964/6361, National Archives of Australia.

11 Spry to Secretary Territories, 19 January 1965, A452 1964/5800, National Archives of Australia.

12 C. R. Ashwin, "Record of Conversation with Mr. Djoko Joewono, Counsellor, Indonesian Embassy on 24th September 1965," A1838 3036/1/4/1/6 part 2, National Archives of Australia.

13 Department of External Affairs, "Notes Prepared as Background Information on the Border between West Irian and the Territory of Papua and New Guinea," 30 September 1969, A1838 932/5/14 part 3, National Archives of Australia.

14 *Commonwealth Parliamentary Debates*, Representatives, vol. 73, 20 August 1971, p. 474.

15 R. Rose to Secretary Territories, 27 June 1966, A1838 932/5/14 part 1, National Archives of Australia.

16 K. Gascoigne, "Application for Permissive Residency Lazarus Michael Itaar – Interviewing Officer's Report on Application," 29 May 1968, A452 1969/1824, National Archives of Australia.

17 Garfield Barwick, Cabinet submission no. 330, 19 July 1962, A1838 3036/14/1/6 part 1, National Archives of Australia.

18 Jack McCarthy, "Refugee 'Prisoners' Live Without Hope," *South Pacific Post*, 21 May 1969.

19 G. A. Jockel to Minister for External Affairs, 30 September 1964, A1838 3036/14/1/6 part 1, National Archives of Australia.

20 G. Warwick Smith to Secretary Department of External Affairs, 8 January 1965, A1838 3036/14/1/6 part 1, National Archives of Australia.

21 Territory Intelligence Committee (T.P.N.G.), "Assessment of Reactions of T.P.N.G. Communities to Influxes of West Irianese Natives," 8 March 1968, A452 1968/2403, National Archives of Australia, Canberra.

22 A. E. Kroker, Mount Gambier Voters' Policy Association to P. Hasluck, 6 June 1965, A1838 3036/14/1/6 part 2, National Archives of Australia, Canberra.

23 H. Lancaster to P. Hasluck, 2 March 1965, A1838 3036/14/1/6 part 2, National Archives of Australia, Canberra.

24 G. C. Lewis, "Record of Conversation – General Suadi and the Minister, on 21st January, 1963," A1838 3036/14/1/6 part 1, National Archives of Australia.

25 *Commonwealth Parliamentary Debates*, Representatives, vol. 36, 23 August 1962, p. 752.

26 Quoted in A. Farran to Jockel, 3 May 1963, A1838 3036/14/1/6 part 1, National Archives of Australia, Canberra. I have been unable to trace the original directive.

27 Hasluck to Secretary, 9 January 1963, A452 1965/8891, National Archives of Australia.

28 R. Marsh, "Policy Regarding Refugees from West New Guinea," 11 March 1964, A452 1963/8261, National Archives of Australia.

29 Charles Edward Barnes, *Commonwealth Parliamentary Debates*, Representatives, vol. 45, 18 May 1965, p. 1553.

30 Local Intelligence Committee (T.P.N.G.), "Monthly Intelligence Summary," no. 6, September 1965, p. 17, A1838 3036/14/1 part 5, National Archives of Australia.

31 A. Besley, file note, 21 February 1969, A452 1969/1177, National Archives of Australia.

32 "Applications for Permissive Residence in T.P.N.G. – Eight West Irianese – Toembay and Others," 19 May 1969, A1838 3036/10/2/2/6, National Archives of Australia.

33 T. A. Byrnes to Commonwealth Director of Migration Brisbane, 28 February 1969, A1838 3036/10/2/2/6, National Archives of Australia.

34 *Commonwealth Parliamentary Debates*, Representatives, vol. 62, 6 March 1969, p. 462.

35 "Interviewing Officer's Report on Application," 11 March 1969, A452 1969/1177, National Archives of Australia.

36 D. O. Hay to Secretary Department of External Territories, 17 April 1969, A452 1969/1177, National Archives of Australia.

37 J. C. G. Kevin to Secretary, 16 April 1958, A1838 TS1606/2 part 1, National Archives of Australia.

Chapter 6: Convention refugees

1 Charles Price, "Australia and Refugees 1921–1976," report commissioned by the National Population Council, May 1990, p. 16.

2 J. B. Chiefly and H. V. Evatt, agendum no. 6950, n.d. (approved by Cabinet 13 May 1947), A2700 695D, National Archives of Australia.

3 T. H. E. Heyes to Secretary Department of External Affairs, 22 May 1950, A1838 855/11/11 part 2, National Archives of Australia.

4 "Conference of Plenipotentiaries on the Status of Refugees and Stateless Persons – Geneva 2nd July, 1951 – Brief for the Australian Delegation," enclosed with A. H. Tange to Minister, 25 June 1951, A1838 855/11/11 part 3, National Archives of Australia.

5 T. H. E. Heyes to Secretary Department of External Affairs, 22 May 1950, A1838 855/11/11 part 2, National Archives of Australia.

6 T. H. E. Heyes to Secretary Department of External Affairs, 23 April 1951, A1838 855/11/11 part 2, National Archives of Australia.

7 United Nations Section, "Draft Convention on the Status of Refugees and

Stateless Persons," 23 May 1951, A1838 855/11/11 part 3, National Archives of Australia.

8 [Patrick Shaw] to Department of External Affairs, 8 July 1951, A1838 855/11/11 part 3, National Archives of Australia.

9 Australian delegation Geneva to Department of External Affairs, 17 July 1951, A1838 855/11/11 part 3, National Archives of Australia.

10 Gil Loescher, *The UNHCR and World Politics: A Perilous Path*, Oxford: Oxford University Press (2001), p. 44.

11 Department of External Affairs to Australian Mission to the United Nations, 4 November 1957, A1838 932/5/3 part 1, National Archives of Australia.

12 Australian Mission to the United Nations to Department of External Affairs, 7 November 1957; Australian Mission to the United Nations to Department of External Affairs, 12 December 1957; both A1838 932/5/3 part 1, National Archives of Australia.

13 Alexander McIver to Secretary Department of External Affairs, 2 March 1965, A1838 932/5/14 part 1, National Archives of Australia.

14 Paul Weis, quoted in Alexander McIver to Furlonger, 19 March 1965, A1838 932/5/14 part 1, National Archives of Australia.

15 R. W. Furlonger to A. McIver, 13 April 1965, A1838 932/5/14 part 1, National Archives of Australia.

16 R. W. Furlonger to B. C. Hill, 13 April 1965, A10034 225/6/18 part 1, National Archives of Australia.

17 B. C. Hill to R. W. Furlonger, 29 April 1965, A10034 225/6/18 part 1, National Archives of Australia.

18 Hill to Department of External Affairs, 23 November 1965, A6980 S251060, National Archives of Australia.

19 Note handed by Felix Schnyder to Brian Hill, 23 November 1965, A10034 225/6/18 part 1, National Archives of Australia.

20 Hill to Department of External Affairs, 13 January 1966, A6980 S251060, National Archives of Australia.

21 See Loescher, *The UNHCR and World Politics*, pp. 245–46.

22 P. Brazil, "Record of Conversation with Dr. A. Rorholt, Legal Adviser to UNHCR, 17 December 1968," A1838 932/5/14 part 3, National Archives of Australia.

23 P. Brazil, "Protocol Relating to the Status of Refugees," 28 November 1968, A1838 929/6/1 part 4, National Archives of Australia.

24 Territories to Administrator, 8 September 1970, A452 1970/3547, National Archives of Australia.

25 Louise W. Holborn, *Refugees: A Problem of Our Time: The Work of the United Nations High Commissioner for Refugees, 1951–1972*, 2 volumes, Methuchen: Scarecrow Press (1975).

Chapter 7: Deportees

1 Abdul Samad bin Amjah to Australian Government Authorities, 24 August 1943, A446 1963/43426, National Archives of Australia.

2 A. C. Palfreeman, *The Administration of the White Australia Policy*, Melbourne: Melbourne University Press (1967), pp. 87–90.

3 Arthur Calwell, quoted in ibid, p. 102.

4 Assistant Secretary to Minister, 22 December 1971, A452 1970/3547, National Archives of Australia.

5 38 men of Java to [Australian Government], 25 June 1946, A518 BI822/1, National Archives of Australia.

6 D. R. Marsh, patrol report no. 3 of 46/47 Daru, 27 August to 26 October 1946, patrol diary and patrol summary, n.d., A518 BI822/1, National Archives of Australia.

7 J. W. Bunton to Secretary External Territories, 28 February 1947, A518 BI822/1, National Archives of Australia.

8 Memorandum to Minister, 8 March 1948, A518 BI822/1, National Archives of Australia.

9 T. H. E. Heyes to Secretary External Territories, 1 June 1949, A518 BI822/1, National Archives of Australia.

10 Nutt to Minister, 21 April 1954, A446 1978/75727, National Archives of Australia.

11 Beilby to Brown, 17 July 1953, A446 1971/60431, National Archives of Australia.

12 Peter Heydon diary, 12 April 1962, MS3155 box 22, folder 184, National Library of Australia.

13 Peter Heydon diary, 13 April 1962, MS3155 box 22, folder 184, National Library of Australia.

14 Richard Hughes, "Wong Did Go by Escort," *Herald*, 16 April 1962.

15 Ann Smith, personal communication, 2 March 2004.

16 David Dutton, *One of Us? A Century of Australian Citizenship*, Sydney: University of New South Wales Press (2002), p. 135.

17 File notes concerning L. and M., n.d. (deportation orders dated 21 June 1950), A6980 S250240, National Archives of Australia.

18 Alexander Downer, *Commonwealth Parliamentary Debates*, Representatives, vol. 36, 10 October 1962, p. 1395.

19 P. R. Heydon to Secretary Attorney-General's Department, 22 May 1963, A432 1974/11015 part 1, National Archives of Australia.

20 "Summary Record of Meeting of 27th July [1967] between Officers of the Department of External Affairs and Territories," p. 2, A1838 3036/14/1/6/1 part 1; H. D. Anderson to Secretary Territories, 13 July 1967, A452 1965/76; both National Archives of Australia.

21 J. M. Starey to Roeslan Soeroso, 20 October 1967, A1838 3036/10/2/2/2, National Archives of Australia.

22 P. J. Galvin, file note, 4 October [1967], A452 1965/76, National Archives of Australia.

23 P. J. Galvin to Secretary Department of External Affairs, 17 January 1968, A1838 3036/14/1/6/1 part 1, National Archives of Australia.

24 Sue Hoffman, "Submission to Immigration Senate Select Inquiry into Ministerial Discretion," n.d. (2003), <www.aph.gov.au/Senate/committee/minmig_ctte/submissions/sub05.doc>.

25 *Commonwealth Parliamentary Debates*, Representatives, 21 August 2002, p. 5390; *Commonwealth Parliamentary Debates*, Representatives, 16 September 2002, pp. 6345–46; Carmen Lawrence, personal communication, 7 October 2003.

26 Administrator to Secretary External Territories, 19 June 1948, A518 BI822/1, National Archives of Australia.

Conclusion

1 E.g. A Just Australia, mission statement, n.d. (2004), <http://www.ajustaustralia.com/ whoweare_whatwedo.php>.

2 E.g. Department of Immigration and Multicultural and Indigenous Affairs, *Refugee and Humanitarian Issues: Australia's Response*, Canberra: Department of Immigration and Multicultural and Indigenous Affairs (2002), p. 7.

3 Quoted in Tony Kushner, "Meaning Nothing But Good: Ethics, History and Asylum-Seeker Phobia in Britain," *Patterns of Prejudice*, vol. 37, no. 3 (2003), p. 273.

4 Kathryn Cronin, "A Culture of Control: An Overview of Immigration Policy Making" in *The Politics of Australian Immigration*, ed. James Jupp and Marie Kabala, Canberra: Australian Government Publishing Service (1993), pp. 83–104.

5 *Commonwealth Parliamentary Debates*, Representatives, 24 May 1977, p. 1714.

Acknowledgements

This book was initially conceived as an essay for A Just Australia. I thank its Director, Howard Glenn, for commissioning the essay, for agreeing to its publication in book form, and for his friendship over the years. I am grateful to the Myer Foundation for funding the writing of the essay through A Just Australia.

I began research on Australia's responses to refugees and asylum seekers when the National Archives of Australia awarded me its Frederick Watson Fellowship in 2001. I thank the then Director-General of the National Archives, Anne-Marie Schwirtlich, for providing me with an incentive to explore the Archives' rich resources, and Archives staff for their crucial support over the past three years. I am particularly grateful to Rod Covell and Michael Wenke and their colleagues in Canberra, Darwin, Adelaide and Sydney, and to the Archives' access examiners (who must think that I have a particular interest in files "not yet examined"). I received further research funding from Swinburne University of Technology's Institute for Social Research in 2002 and the Northern Territory History Grants Committee in 2003, and thank both.

Earlier versions of parts of this book appeared in *Australian Historical Studies* (vol. 33, no. 120) and *Australian Journal of Human Rights* (vol. 9, no. 2). I thank Joy Damousi and Ian Hunt for their respective invitations to commit my ideas to paper.

I am indebted to Peter Mares and Roger Averill for carefully reading the manuscript and for their many constructive suggestions, and to Kate Manton for being as exacting and sympathetic an editor as any author could wish for. The book would be poorer without their input, but of course responsibility for all its shortcomings rests with me.

Finally, I would like to thank Susanna and Claudio for tolerating the long working hours that were associated with this project.

— *Klaus Neumann, 12 April 2004*